Are They?

They Do Not Understand Series

Patricia C. Vines

Copyright @2016

Patricia C. Vines

All rights reserved. No part of this book may be reproduced or transmitted in any form or by any means, electronic or mechanical, including photocopying, recording, or by any information storage and retrieval system, without permission in writing from the copyright owner or author.

The information in this book is for educational purposes only.

ISBN-13: 978-1530055753
ISBN-10: 153005575X

First Edition
Published; March 2016
Printed in the United States of America

Table of Contents

Introduction iv
Acknowledgments vii
Eve 1
Women Who Were Not A Proverbs 31 Woman 20
   Potiphar's Wife 20
   Rahab 24
   Gomer 26
   Delilah 28
   Jezebel 31
   Herodias And Salome 33
   Cunning And Deceptive Women ....
   Rebekah 37
   Tamar, Daughter-in-law of Judah 40
   Women Of Jeremiah 44 Were Not Proverbs 31 Women 45
Beautiful Women Of The Bible 48
   Abigail 48
   Rahab 53
   Esther 54
   Sarah And Rebekah 58
   Sarah 59
   Daughters Of Job 61
Women Who Didn't Start Off As A Proverbs 31 Woman But Grew Into One
   Bathsheba 62
   Rachel 65
Wedding Traditions From The Bible 66
Women Of Strength And Courage ....
   Deborah 67
   The Bleeding Woman 69
   Ruth 71
Gleaning 74
   Jochebed – Mother of Moses 74
Remarkable Women (Mothers) 74
   Hannah 77
   Lois And Eunice 79
   Sarah 81
Widow At Nain 81

Canaanite Woman	83
Women Who Sang The Blues	85
Hagar	85
Tamar – Daughter Of King David	88
Leah	90
Woman Whom Solomon Loved	
Abishag	95
Woman In The House Of Simon The Pharisee	96
Women Whom Met Jesus And Loved	
Mary and Martha	98
The Samaritan Woman At The Well	100
The Woman Caught In The Act of Adultery	102
Women At The Tomb Of Jesus	104
Mary Magdalene	104
Joanna	107
Mary – Mother Of James And Joses	108
Salome	109
The Mother of Jesus	109
Elizabeth	110
Mary, The Mother Of Jesus	113
The Immaculate Conception	116
Proverbs 31	120
7 Feast Of The LORD Being Symbolic Of New Life	122
Bibliography	123

Introduction

I am going to present to you (each reader) a fascinating and inspiring stories of the most blessed and unblessed women of all times. Some are Proverbs 31 Women, some are not, some border on being, some not. It is the story of mothers and women which spent time with Jesus (Yeshua) and the apostles. It is the stories of the beautiful, the cunning, the courageous and the abused women of the Bible. Here will be stories of the women whom were mothers of many children. That brought women honor, love and security. An inability to have children was a sigma of the worst kind, it was a stigma that Sarah, Rachel and Hannah all bore until God allowed them to conceive.

In the Old Testament, the father (husband) made decisions for the family and women had very little to say about it. Women did not have the same legal rights as men (a man could divorce his wife, but a wife could not divorce her husband). Women received their security and identity from their husbands and, with a few exceptions, were not in positions of leadership: men – not women – offered sacrifices to God. In the Torah, Leviticus 27 suggests that a woman was worth only half as much as a man.

Leviticus 27: 1-8 - "And the Lord spoke unto Moses, saying, Vs. 2 – Speak unto the children of Israel, and say unto them. When a man shall make a special vow, the persons SHALL BE for the LORD by thy "valuation." Vs. 3 – "And thy "valuation" shall be of the male from twenty (20) years old, even unto sixty (60) years old, even thy "valuation" shall be fifty (50) shekels of silver, after the shekel of the sanctuary. Vs. 4 – "And if it BE a female, then thy "valuation" shall be thirty (30) shekels. Vs. 5 – "And if it BE from five (5) years old, then thy "valuation" shall BE of the male twenty (20) shekels, and for the female ten (10) shekels. Vs. 6 – "And if it BE from

a month old, even unto five (5) years old, then thy "valuation" shall BE of the male five (5) shekels of silver, and for the female thy "valuation" shall BE three (3) shekels of silver. Vs. 7 – "And if it BE from sixty (60) and above, if it BE a male, then thy "valuation" shall be fifteen (15) shekels and for the female ten (10) shekels. Vs. 8 - "But if be poorer than thy "valuation", then he shall present himself before the priest, and the priest shall "value" him; according to his ability who vowed shall the priest "value" him." Read on through the remaining verses of Leviticus concerning "valuation". Leviticus 27:9-25 regarded things. Leviticus 27:26-27 regarded "Three (3) things that are the LORD'S absolutely: (1) firstlings of the beasts. Leviticus 27:28-29 regarded "Any dedicated thing" and Leviticus 27: 30-34 regarded "All tithes of land, tree and beast."

Yeshua (Jesus) is The Rose of Sharon.

Song of Solomon 2:1;
1 I *am* the rose of Sharon, *and* the lily of the valley.

Acknowledgments

GOD'S WORD® Translation is a registered trademark of GOD'S WORD® to the Nations, PO Box 400, Orange Park, Florida 32067-0400.

"Scripture quotations taken from the New American Standard Bible®, Copyright© 1960, 1962, 1963, 1968, 1971, 1972, 1973, 1975, 1977, 1995 by The Lockman Foundation Used by permission." (www.Lockman.org)

Scripture quotations are taken from the HOLY BIBLE, New Living Translation, copyright© 1996, 2004, 2007, 2013 by Tyndale House Foundation. Used by permission of Tyndale House Publishers, Inc., Carol Stream, Illinois 60188. All rights reserved.

Some of the Scripture quotations, in this publication are from the HOLY BIBLE, NEW INTERNATIONAL VERSION® NIV® Copyright© 1973, 1978, 1984, 2011 by Biblica, Inc.®. Used by permission. All rights reserved worldwide. The "NIV" and "New International Version" are trademarks registered in the United States Patent and Trademark Office by Biblica, Inc.®. Use of either trademark requires the permission of Biblica, Inc.®.

"Scripture quotations are from The Holy Bible, English Standard Version® (ESV®), copyright© 2001 by Crossway, a publishing ministry of Good News Publishers. Used by permission. All rights reserved."

Scripture quotations marked HCSB are taken from the Holman Christian Standard Bible®, Copyright© 1999, 2000, 2002, 2003 by Holman Bible Publishers. Used by permission. Holman Christian Standard Bible®, Holman CSB®, and HCSB® are federally registered trademarks of Holman Bible Publishers.

Scripture taken from the New King James Version®. Copyright© 1982 by Thomas Nelson, Inc. Used by permission. All rights reserved.

All pictures and information contained therein in this book is factual to the best of the authors information and is presented for informational and entertainment purposes only.

Eve

Throughout the Scriptures you will notice something striking that "Female characters abound. And it is not simply a lot of women; it is about a lot of "strong" women. These women are... not passive, timid and submissive, but active, bold, fearless and assertive. You will note that in the first chapters of Genesis it makes it quite clear that women as well as men were created in the "image of God". In the Old Testament for women "wisdom" is personified, but, in the New Covenant, Jesus (Yeshua) treated women and men equally. When he asked a Samaritan woman for a drink, he broke down all racial, gender and religious barriers.

As you may or may not be familiar with all the women of Scripture - I will strive to break the women down into different categories and chapters, beginning with Eve.

Genesis 2:15
"And the Lord God said, 'It is not good that man should be alone; I will make him a helper comparable to him.'"

So God made all the animals and birds and brought them to the man. But no animal was a suitable companion for the man.

Genesis 2:21-22
"And the Lord God caused a deep sleep to fall on Adam, and he slept; and he took one of his ribs (spine) and closed up the flesh in its place. Then the rib which the Lord God had taken from man he made into a woman, and he brought her to the man."

Eve was violently and passionately pulled out of Adam. Eve may have cried then because she did not understand why she was there and did not know what she was to do. She was just like a new born baby.

Genesis 2:23-25
"And Adam said: 'This is now bone of my bones and flesh of my flesh; she shall be called woman, because she was taken out of man.'
"Therefore a man shall leave his father and mother and be joined to his wife, and they shall become one flesh.
And they were both naked, the man and his wife, and were not ashamed."

There are actually two accounts of the creation of man and woman. The first is rather general; the second is more specific.

The first chapter of Genesis says, **"Then God said, 'And now we will make human beings; they will be like us and resemble us. They will have power over the fish, the birds, and all animals, domestic and wild, large and small.'** So God created human beings, making them to be like himself. He created them male and female, blessed them, and said, **'Have many children, so that your descendants will live all over the earth and bring it under their control. I am putting you in charge of the fish, the birds, and all the wild animals. I have provided all kinds of grain and all kinds of fruit for you to eat; but for all the wild animals and for all the birds I have provided grass and leafy plants for food'** and it was done. God looked at everything he had made, and he was very pleased." (Good News Translation)

Neither Adam nor Eve was mentioned by name. Each one alone was incomplete; together they made up humankind. God created both man and woman **"to be like himself,"** or, as the familiar King James Version of the Bible says, **"in the image of God."**

The second account of the creation of man and woman is in Chapter 2. Here God created man first **"out of dirt (dust) from the ground and blew into his nostrils the breath of** life. **The man came alive-a living soul!"** God then planted a garden in Eden and put the man in it. Specifically mentioned are the **"tree of life"** and the **"tree of the knowledge of good and evil."** God said about the tree of the knowledge of good and evil, **"Don't eat from it. The moment you eat from that tree, you're dead." Scripture from "The Message" by Eugene H. Peterson, 1993.**

It was only then, after making plants and animals and putting the man in the garden, that God made the woman by taking her from the man. Adam was suppose to protect Eve but did not because he did not understand what was happening.

The story continues. The serpent asked the woman if God had said she and the man could eat the fruit of the trees. The only prohibition, she replied, was the tree in the middle of the garden. If they touched it or ate it, they would die. **"That's not true; you will not die,"** the serpent said. **"God said that because he knows that when you eat it, you will be like God and know what is good and what is bad (evil)."** The serpent (hasatan), the devil, tempted Eve with "wisdom" in Genesis 3:6. Wisdom concerning evil. Who was the tempter? satan, the serpent. He is wise but his wisdom is not godly. Perhaps he was being referred to by the Messiah when He told His talmidim (disciples) to be **"wise as serpents and harmless as doves."** Matthew 10:16 says, **"Behold, I send you forth as sheep in the midst of wolves; by ye, therefore, wise as serpents, and harmless as doves.** So the woman ate the fruit, gave some to her husband and **"as soon as they had eaten it, they were given understanding and realized that they were naked; so they sewed fig leaves together and covered themselves."** Once the fruit was digested and entered the blood stream, the deed was done.

Eve ate of the fruit because she was deceived and did not understand. Adam was not deceived. God gave Adam the command "to not eat" long before Eve was ever formed. And neither one of them took responsibility for their actions. They played the blame game.

The first sin is highly significant because it's the first. But the second sin may, in fact, be more important-because we will never recover from the first sin so long as we are guilty of the second. The Scriptures and human experience both testify that God has provided a remedy for the first sin, no matter what it is. Yeshua whom paid the price to bring us out of the "slave market of sin." But the second sin can make God's remedy ineffective. Looking back at Scripture we will see how it happened. After Adam and Eve had eaten the forbidden fruit, they became ashamed of their nakedness; but far more important, they became **"Uneasy" with God.** So, when God came walking in the Garden soon thereafter, they tried to hide from God Yeshua. They must have realized that it is impossible to hide from Yeshua (God), but sin causes us humans to do irrational things: sin is never very smart, you know, not even when it dresses itself in sophistication. **"Why are you hiding?"** God asked. And Adam who had been quite silent in the conversations with the serpent, replied, **"I heard you coming and didn't want you to see me naked. So I hid."**

WELL, HELLO!!! God knew and He pressed the matter. **"Who told you that you were naked? Have you eaten fruit from the tree about which I warned you?"** Adam answered, **"Yes, but it was the woman you gave me who brought me some, and I ate it!"** And Eve, not to be left bearing sole responsibility, chimed in. **"The serpent tricked me."** Now, we have the second sin and it is even more dangerous than the first, because it prevents us from recovering from the first. It is the sin of **"EXCUSES"** the unwillingness to admit that we are wrong and the refusal to see ourselves for what we really are. Whatever our original sin may be, whether it is lying, adultery, cheating, ill temper, gluttony, drunkenness, gossip, or murder, there is always hope for us. But when we become guilty of the second sin, the sin of excusing ourselves and of being unwilling to face ourselves, we close the door against God and hope. I have suggested that the second sin may be what is called "the unpardonable sin." The unpardonable sin is defined as the sin against the Holy Spirit, **Mark 3:28, 29 - "Verily I say unto you, All sins shall be forgiven unto the sons of men, and blasphemies with which they shall blaspheme; Vs. 29 – But he that shall blaspheme against the Holy spirit hath never forgiveness, but is in danger of eternal damnation;** this explains a blaspheming of the Spirit of God. The Holy Spirit is the persuasive agent in our lives, the power which convicts us of sin. When we excuse ourselves and refuse to recognize our sins, we harden ourselves against the Spirit's work of persuasion. This very act of resisting and hardening is a sin against the Spirit, a blaspheming so to speak, of the Spirit's work. How could we be more lost than to be in a state where we are no longer disturbed about being wrong? We come to such a place by the continuing process of self-excusing.

We are experts in hiding from the knowledge of what we are! Adam and Eve set the pattern for us, and we have been refining it ever since. When God asked Adam if he had eaten from the forbidden tree, he had the opportunity to step forward and confess what he had done. Instead he answered. "Yes, BUT the woman.... What a courageous soul he was: brave, ready to shoulder responsibility! "It was the woman!!!!!" It must also be said that man led the way to the second sin. And in both cases, the other was all too prompt to follow. And Eve would excuse her failure with, "The devil made me do it." But Adam's excuse did not stop with shifting the burden of blame to Eve. He complains to God, *"It was the woman YOU (Yeshua) gave me."* In other words, **"It's ALL your fault, God, for so generously providing me with this lovely creature who led me astray-this one of whom I said so recently that she was bone of my bone and flesh of my flesh. It's YOUR fault for giving her to me."**

Adam was furious. We have been talking to God this way ever since. **"It's the temperament you gave me. I can't help myself." "It is in my genes." "It is my lack of talent." " If only Yeshua had given me more talent."** We are quite sure we can find the secrets in our genetic code to prove that we are really not responsible for what we do. Please know that there is NO truth in hasatan (satan). The TRUTH is in the Word and Words of God.

God can visit the penitent soul because the penitent soul has an open door. But God is shut out of the life that covers over its failure with a hard surface of EXCUSES. The Forgiving One never has opportunity to forgive and restore those who will not acknowledge that they want such a divine Friend whom is full of "grace" and "Mercy." Whatever we do with this life, whatever course we follow, let us be sure that we do not die making excuses.

When God confronted the man and woman, the man blamed the women: **"The woman you gave me as a companion, she gave me fruit from the tree, and yes, I ate it."** Some might say that men have been blaming women ever since. The woman tried to pass the blame as well. **"The serpent seduced me."** she said, **"and I ate." (The Message)** They did not understand and still do not understand. But women have not been as successful as men in getting the transfer of their blame to stick.

God put a curse on the serpent. He then told the woman she would experience pain in childbirth, and that she would be subject to her husband. And he told the man that the ground would be cursed because of him and he **"will have to work hard all your life to make it produce enough food for you."** God then expelled them from the garden, in order that they would not have access to the tree of life. Eve then gave birth to Cain and Abel. Abel committed the first murder, and Eve became the first mother to grieve the death of a child. She also had the heartache of knowing that her other son, Cain, was a murderer. Adam and Eve then gave birth to Seth (whom was to be the line for the birth of our Saviour-Yeshua) and they also gave birth to **"other sons and daughters."**

According to the story in Genesis, Eve ate the fruit of the tree of knowledge of good and evil. But just as Eve was tempted to eat the fruit, there are those who interpret the Bible are tempted to leave things obscure or vague. The fruit was said to be: A fig because Adam and Eve covered themselves with fig leaves. Grapes because wine was thought to be a drink of the gods. Wheat because the Hebrew word is similar to that for "sin." A carob because the Hebrew word is similar to that for "destruction." Nuts because nuts were thought to be an aphrodisiac. Most popular is the apple. It was first identified as the fruit Eve ate by a Christian poet about 1,500 years ago. The apple's red color says "danger," but the inside is delicious, sweet and tempting. The primary reason is probably that the Latin word for "apple" and the Latin word for an "evil" or misfortune" are the same: "malum." And once the apple caught on, it was pictured in medieval and modern paintings, and became a popular interpretation by both Christians and Jews. Lets please stop giving the apple a bad rap. The fruit was not an apple.

The truth is: By the disobedience of ONE man, sin entered the world. Adam.

We know what the knowledge of good and evil are, so.

The question is? What does Proverbs 31 have to do with 1 Corinthians, chapter 13 and woman. That is a great question. The answer is far more than you realize. I will connect most of the verses in Chapter 13 to Proverbs 31 as taught in Torah. The Proverb 31 woman understands and seeks out more understanding because she realizes "love" is about all... literally. The following verse confirms this thinking.

1 Corinthians 13:13
**13 And now these three remain: faith, hope and love. But

the greatest of these is love.

Christians quote this concept over and over again. But do they REALLY understand it? They say it is the love of Christ. That is the new law. But what does that mean? If you were to ask them to explain what the love of Christ is, as our Righteous Heavenly Father definition of it is, can they answer it? Can anyone reading this book answer that question? Can you point to the verses which back it up? I am not trying to put any reader on the "spot" necessarily. I am just asking the question. Beloved, this is the meat of the Word. This is not milk. Knowing these things help us grow. Grow into maturity as Paul states in his teachings. The goal is that you may begin to apply these concepts in your life. When it comes right down to it, it is a heart issue. Father clearly explains this over and over again.

Deuteronomy 10:15-16
15 Yet the Lord set his affection on your ancestors and loved them, and he chose you, their descendants, above all the nations, as it is today.
16 **Circumcise** your hearts, therefore, and do not be stiff-necked any longer.

I would imagine everyone reading this book wants to come into the knowledge of the truth. Let's approach all this learning as if we are learning it for the first time. In my opinion, we need and should be teachable and willing to be open to re-evaluating everything we think we know. Again, we are not interested in BEING right, it is about GETTING it right. If you want change - change things in your life. Let's learn the right things. Keep in mind, we quoted the verse "13, And now these three remain: faith, hope and love. But the greatest of these is love." But do we REALLY understand the depth of it? What is interesting is the verse I just wrote is above this next verse.

Hebrews 11:6
6 And without faith it is impossible to please God, because anyone who come to him must believe that He exists and that He rewards those who earnestly seek him.

As important as faith in the God of Abraham, Isaac, and Jacob is, the much bigger item in the picture is loving. We need to really grasp a hold of what Father says is LOVE. Not what the world says it is in movies, soap operas, teachings, fiction love stories, etc.

I will be connecting passages to Proverbs 31. In some cases, you have multiple verses which can be applied. Then there are concepts which Proverbs 31 teach which will apply also. So, if there is a link to 1 Corinthians 13, keep in mind there could be other verses which could also fit.

I am stating the first four verses. And then explain starting with verse 4 in 1 Corinthians 13.

1 Corinthians 13:1-4
1 If I could speak all the languages of earth and of angels, but didn't love others, I would only be a noisy gong or a clanging cymbal.
2 If I had the gift of prophecy and if I understood all of God's secret plans and possessed all knowledge, and if I had such faith that I could move mountains, but did not love other, I would be nothing.
3 If I gave everything I have to the poor and even sacrificed my body, I could boast about it, but if I didn't love others, I would have gained nothing.
4 Love is **patient**, love is kind. It does not envy, it does not boast, it is not proud.

The first thing that we are going to focus on is: **Patient**. In the Greek, that word patient means: to suffer long, am forbearing, perseverance, refusing to retaliate with anger, because of human reasoning, "long-suffering" because it only expresses anger as the Lord directs. It is the opposite of being "quick-tempered."

Let's get down to the nitty-gritty. How many times have you heard someone say, "I'm not a patient person" or "I'm not patient with this person when they do this or that" or "I'm not patient with someone who thinks this way or that way" or "I do not pray for patience because it brings tribulation." How many times have you heard someone say those things and others like it? Yet that is the very first thing Paul says. **"Love is patient."** We do not understand do we, yet?

Here are some practical applications for being patient. We can be patient with our children and our teenagers when they do not do what we tell them to do. Our parents or grandparents when they get involved in our personal business when we do not want their input. How about our neighbors, friends, co-workers. I am sure many of you have the picture(s) of people who, shall I say, try your patience; right? (pun intended). We all have stories to tell. We can be here all day reading about them, right? But we are supposed to be patient. A Proverbs 31 woman is patient. She understands these things. Patience brings calm into your and her life and those who are around her. She knows when someone wants her advice and when they do not. She is not hurt of offended when they do not want it. She does not volunteer it (casting pearls among those who will leave it on the ground to be trampled on) either unless she feels inspired by the LORD to speak.

Let us go up one level. If you love, you are patient, are you ready, with YOURSELF. Are you patient with yourself? Be honest. Sometimes we set the bar up so high that if we miss it. When and if that happens we beat ourselves up because we did not make the standard. We think that is spiritual. Well, beloved, everything is SPIRITUAL, if you believe it or not. If you are not patient with yourself, then you are not loving yourself. A Proverbs 31 woman is patient with herself. She understands the value of being in that state of mind. Are we getting this? You need to BE PATIENT with YOURSELF! I am not talking about hiding behind excuses either.

The Proverbs 31 link is verse 12.

Proverbs 31:12
12 She helps him and never harms him all the days of her life.

Here are the links to the Torah for patience:

Exodus 34:8
8 And the LORD passed by before him, and proclaimed, the LORD, The LORD God, merciful and gracious, long-suffering, and abundant in goodness and truth.

Numbers 14:18
18 The LORD *is* long-suffering, and of great mercy, forgiving iniquity and transgression, and by no means clearing *the guilty,* visiting he iniquity of the fathers upon the children unto he third and fourth *generation (curses).*

Learn to move into being more and more patient with others and yourself.

KIND
4 Love is patient, **love is KIND.** It does not envy, it does not boast, it is not proud.

In the Greek, that word "kind" means; I am kind (full of service to others), gentle.
If you love, you are gentle and full of service to others no matter what they do to you or your loved ones. Here is what Yeshua (Jesus) says about it. He is really quoting Torah.

Matthew 5:43-48

43 "You have heard that it was said, 'Love your neighbor and hate your enemy.'
44 But I tell you, love your enemies and pray for those who persecute you.
45 That you may be children of your Father in Heaven. He causes his sun to rise on the evil and the good, and sends rain on the righteous and the unrighteous.
46 If you love those who love you, what reward will you get? Are not even the tax collectors doing that?
47 And if you greet only your own people, what are you doing more than others? Do not even pagans do that?
48 Be perfect, therefore as your heavenly Father is perfect.

The next level is: are you ready? Are you kind to YOURSELF? If you are not kind to yourself, you are beating yourself up. Some people might think that makes you humble. That mindset is not spiritual. As I stated "All things are spiritual." We are also supposed to be kind to others as we are to ourselves.

The Proverbs 31 line is verse 20.

Proverbs 21:20
20 She opens her hands to oppressed people and stretches them out to needy people.

Here is the link to Torah and to the Renewed Testament.

Leviticus 25:35
35 "If any of your fellow Israelites become poor and are unable to support themselves among you, help them as you would a foreigner and stranger, so they can continue to live among you.

Romans 12:19
19 Dearly beloved, avenge not yourselves, but *rather* give place unto wrath: for it is written, Vengeance *is* mine; I will repay saith the Lord.

Deuteronomy is actually being quoted here from the verse above in Romans.

Deuteronomy 32:35
35 To me *belongeth* vengeance, and recompence; their foot shall slide in *due* time: for the day of their calamity *is* at hand, and the things that shall come upon them make haste.

According to what Yeshua (Jesus) said, how blessed we are if we actually do the things we are taught to do from the Word.

John 13:17
17 Now that you know these things, you will be blessed if you do them.

Like the word "Shema." Hear and obey what you read and or hear.

Envy
4 Love is patient, love is kind. **It does not ENVY,** it does not boast, it is not proud.

In the Greek, that word "envy" means; I am jealous, becoming jealous, I am jealous of a person, I am eager to poses a person or a thing. To desire earnestly, eagerly seek, eagerly sought, earnestly desire, envious. Interesting isn't it?
If you notice, it is all about acquiring things, status, or people. It is what you get for yourself. It is not what you can get and give to others.

Proverbs 31:20
20 She opens her hands to oppressed people and stretches them out to needy people.

In the Torah, here you have Joseph's brothers starting to be jealous of him. His brothers would eventually sell him into slavery as a result. Here is one example why we are not to envy others.

Genesis 37:11
11 And his brethren envied him; but his Father observed the saying.

Boast
4 Love is patient, love is kind. It does not envy, **it does not BOAST,** it is not proud.

In the Greek, that word "boast" means I boast, count myself, "a braggart", to act as a braggart, a "show off" who needs too much attention. How many times have we been wanting to be the center of attention? So they can hear our stories of pain and suffering; tales of woe. When we had people who would listen, we would make sure you can vent on them. Yet when others offered solutions to help possibly solve some of their problems, their counsel is ignored. And we continue talking. It is almost those tales of woe is something we want to hang onto. Yet, a Proverbs 31 woman knows where that leads and breaks the chains of bondage so a higher level of freedom is achieved.

A Proverbs 31 woman lets others brag on her. You won't hear that on her lips very often if at all. She is focused on doing what needs to be done, not on the awards she will receive. She knows that talking too much to others does not serve her well. She knows being the center of attention is not always needed. She will be confident when she is the center of attention. But she never seeks it for herself. She knows she needs to listen to others so they can be helped. When that happens, she can rest assured her needs will be taken care of.

Here are the verses in Proverbs.

Proverbs 31:11-12
11 Her husband trusts her with (all) his heart, and he does not lack anything good.

12 She helps him and never harms him all the days of her life.

Here is the verse in the Torah for you.

Deuteronomy 8:17
17 And thou say in thine heart, My power and the might of *mine* hand hath gotten me this wealth.

Proud
4 Love is patient, love is kind. It does not envy, it does not boast, **it is not proud.**

In the Greek, that word "proud" means I inflate, puff up; I am puffed up, arrogant, proud, inflate by blowing; (figuratively) swelled up, like an egotistical person spewing out arrogant ("puffed-up") thoughts. You won't hear those things coming from a Proverbs 31 woman. She is confident and knows who she is. She increases her wisdom and enhances who she is all the time.

Proverbs 31:15
15 She wakes up while it is still dark and gives food to her family and portions of food to her female slaves.

In the Torah it mentions being proud.

Leviticus 26:18-19
18 And if ye will not yet for all this hearken unto me, then I will punish you seven times more for your sins.
19 And I will break the pride of your power; and I will make your Heaven as iron, and your earth as brass.

1 Corinthians 13:5
5 It does not dishonor others, it is not self-seeking, it is not easily angered, it keeps no record of wrongs.

Rude or dishonor others

In the Greek, that word "dishonor" means act improperly, am unseemly, behave unbecomingly (or even dishonorably); perhaps: I consider (something) unseemly, "without proper shape, form", to act unseemly (literally, "improperly"); (figuratively) to lack proper form and hence thought of as unseemly.

Proverbs 31:28-29
28 Her children and her husband stand up and bless her. In addition, he sings her praises, by saying,
29 'Many women have done noble work, but you have surpassed them all!'

In the Torah it mentions being rude or dishonoring others.

Exodus 23:9
9 Also thou shalt not oppress a stranger: for ye know the heart of a stranger, seeing ye were strangers in the land of Egypt.

Self seeking
5 It does not dishonor others, **it is not self-seeking,** it is not easily angered, it keeps no record of wrongs.

In the Greek, that word "self-seeking" means self searching for, self desire, require, self demand. I seek, I search for, I desire, I require, I demand.
In the Torah it is mentioned in;

Numbers 14:29
29 Your carcasses shall fall in this wilderness; and all that were numbered of you, according to your whole number, from twenty years old and upward, which have murmured against me.

Not easily angered.
5 It does not dishonor others, it is no self-seeking, it is **not easily angered,** it keeps no record of wrongs.

In the Greek, that word "easily angered" means properly, cut close alongside, to incite ("jab") someone and stimulate their feelings (emotions); "become emotionally provoked (upset, *roused to anger)*" as *personally* "getting to someone"; (figuratively) *"to provoke feelings, spurring* someone to action."
In the Torah it is mentioned in;

Exodus 34:6
6 And he passed in front of Moses, proclaiming, "The LORD, the LORD, the compassionate and gracious God, slow to anger, abounding in love and faithfulness.

Keeps no record of wrongs, hold grudge(s)
5 It does not dishonor others, it is no self-seeking, it is not easily angered, it **keeps no record of wrongs.**

In the Greek, the word "record" means reckon, count, charge with: reason, decide, concluder, think, suppose, properly, *compute,* "take into account", *reckon* (come to a "bottom-line"). It is referring to something that was done and put down somewhere.
In the Greek, the word "wrongs" means bad, evil, in the widest sense. ("inner malice"), properly, inwardly *foul, rotten (poisoned); (*figuratively) inner *malice* flowing out of a *morally-rotten* character (the "rot is already in the wood").
In the Torah it mentioned.

Leviticus 19:18
18 Thou shalt not avenge, nor bear any grudge against the children of thy people, but thou shalt love thy neighbor as thyself: I **am** the LORD.

1 Corinthians 13:6
6 Rejoiceth not in iniquity, but rejoiceth in the truth.

In the Torah it is mentioned in;

Exodus 18:9
9 And Jethro rejoiced for all the goodness which the LORD had done to Israel, whom he had delivered out of the hand of the Egyptians.

1 Corinthians 13:7
7 Beareth all things, believeth all things, hopeth all things, endureth all things.

Bears
In the Greek, the word "bears" means cover, conceal, ward off, bear with, endure patiently, to place under *roof,* to *cover-over* (with a roof); (figuratively) to *endure* because *shielded,* i.e. Bearing up (forbearing) because under *the Lord's protection (covering).*

In the Torah it is mentioned;

Exodus 18:23
23 If thou dost this, thou shalt fulfill the commandment of God, and shalt be able to bear his precepts: and all this people shall return to their places with peace.

Believes
7 Beareth all things, **believeth all things**, hopeth all things, endureth all things.

In the Greek, the word "believes" means have faith in, trust in; I am entrusted with. "Persuade, be persuaded, affirm, have confidence; used of persuading oneself and with the sacred significance of being persuaded by the Lord.

In the Torah it is mentioned in;

Deuteronomy 1:30-32
30 The LORD your God which goeth before you, he shall fight for you, according to all that he did for you in Egypt before your eyes;
31 And in the wilderness, where thou hast seen how that the LORD thy God bare thee, as a man doth bear his son, in all the way that ye went, until ye came into this place.
32 Yet in this thing ye did not believe the LORD your God.

Hope
7 Beareth all things, believeth all things, **hopeth all things,** endureth all things.

In the Greek, the word "hope" means expect, trust, *actively waiting* for God's fulfillment about the faith.
In the Torah it is mentioned in;

Genesis 49:18
18 "I wait with hope for you to rescue me, O LORD.

Endure
7 Beareth all things, believeth all things, hopeth all things, **endureth all things.**

In the Greek, the word "endures" means remain behind, stand my ground, bear up against, persevere, literally, *remaining under* (the load), bearing up.
In the Torah it is mentioned in;

Numbers 14:27
27 How long must I endure this evil community that keeps complaining about Me? I have heard the Israelites' complaints that they make against Me.

1 Corinthians 13:8
6 Love never fails. But where there are prophecies, they will cease; where there are tongues, they will be stilled; where

there is knowledge, it will pass away.

In the Torah it is mentioned in;

Deuteronomy 31:6
6 Be strong and of good courage, fear not, nor be afraid of them: for the LORD thy God, he it is that doth go with thee; he will not fail thee, nor forsake thee.

Deuteronomy 31:8
8 And the LORD, he *it is* that doth go before thee; he will be with thee, he will not fail thee, neither forsake thee: fear not, neither be dismayed.

Women Who Were Not A Proverbs 31 Woman

God is a God of redemption and restoration. Was He able to restore and redeem the following women?

Following are the stories of many women that may or may not have been "cunning and deceptive" women in the Scriptures.

Potiphar's Wife
As Captain of the Palace Guard, Potiphar was away from home a great deal, so he was pleased when the young Hebrew, (Joseph), slave he purchased from Midianite traders turned out so well. Joseph started out doing menial tasks such as baking bread, butchering cattle and tending the gardens. Potiphar gave him more and more responsibility until finally he turned over the management of the house to Joseph. It was unusual for a slave to be so honest, conscientious and obedient.

Their home was surrounded by a wall for safety and privacy. A small temple, formal gardens and an ornamental pond greeted any visitor. The ground floor contained servants' quarters and workrooms. The family lived on the second floor. The elegance and splendor was foreign to the young Israelite, Joseph, because his family lived in tents and herded sheep.

Potiphar's Wife was well built and good looking. Possibly she did not set out to be an adulteress. What were the circumstances that allowed her to insist on Joseph adapting to her wants, desires? She was obviously in a state of sheer unhappiness and miserable. She was energized enough to decide that Joseph was extremely good-looking and desirable physically. Maybe he was the only man available at the time and she was lonely or bored. Perhaps her Mother had done the same thing and she saw no wrong in it or her Father never taught her Torah because he worshiped so many tens of hundreds of gods (pagan). She was not a Proverbs 31 woman or she would have never considered the possibility of sex with the servant. A person she considered lower than herself in status. Perhaps this had happened before, having few principles of morality and she "got away with it" without her husband's knowledge or did he? If he did know, did he care? Clearly Mrs. Potiphar did not have enough to do around the house. Her husband had given her everything she needed- except, himself. She enjoyed whatever she wanted, and she decided that she wanted Joseph, she may have decided as I said earlier that she was very lonely and that he would or might fulfill the loneliness. Maybe he could fulfill what her husband had not. Every wife is an extension of her husband in another body and Mr. Potiphar possibly failed to love his wife appropriately. She said to Joseph, **"Sleep with me."** Joseph refused and said: **"Potiphar has put me in charge of everything he owns... How could I violate his trust and sin against God?"** Joseph's rejection only made him more desirable and Mrs. Potiphar was persistent in her lust. One day when she knew everyone would be gone, she prepared herself for love. When Joseph walked into her room, she grabbed him and said, **"...sleep with me."** Joseph ran out of the house, leaving his loincloth in her hands. She did not understand that Joseph had been raised to obey, love, worship and honor the God of Abraham, Isaac and Jacob and there was NO other. He was loyal.

Hell hath no fury like a woman scorned. First she told the servants Joseph had tried to seduce her, and then she confronted Potiphar. **"That Hebrew slave that "you" brought here came into my room and insulted me. But when I screamed, he ran outside, leaving his robe beside me."**

Potiphar became so angry with his trusted servant that he had Joseph put in jail. In his heart he may have realized that his wife was lying to save her own skin, so to speak, but he must have sensed something because he did not have Joseph put to death, which was his right as Captain of the Guard.

Mrs. Potiphar's wife was furious because she wanted Joseph put to death, secretly to cover up her desires and lies. Did this "drama" cause her to live a more moral and trustworthy life with her husband. We will never really know except to hope that is what took place. Then, when Joseph was eventually made second in command of Egypt, how did she feel, knowing he knew the truth? We need to realize how God preserved Joseph's life as He (Yeshua) had sent him to Egypt to preserve a nation and that hasatan's scheme did not work. The point of this story is to show the virtue of Joseph. When he landed in jail, his integrity, trustworthiness and honesty eventually put him in charge not just of the household of an Egyptian court official but in charge of all of Egypt, second in power to Pharaoh.

Genesis 39:1-20
1 And Joseph was brought down to Egypt; and Potiphar, an officer of Pharaoh, captain of the guard, an Egyptian, bought him of the hands of the Ishmaelites, which had brought him down thither.
2 And the LORD was with Joseph, and he was a prosperous man; and he was in the house of his master the Egyptian.
3 And his master saw that the LORD *was* with him, and that

the LORD made all that he did to prosper in his hand.
4 And Joseph found grace in his sight, and he served him: and he made him overseer over his house, and all that he had he put into his hand.
5 And it came to pass from the time *that* he had made him overseer in his house, and over all that he had, that the LORD blessed the Egyptian's house for Joseph's sake; and the blessing of the LORD was upon all that he had in the house, and in the field.
6 And he left all that he had in Joseph's hand; and he knew not ought he had, save the bread which he did eat. And Joseph was *a* goodly *person*, and well favored.
7 And it came to pass after these things, that his master's wife cast her eyes upon Joseph; and she said, Lie with me.
8 But he refused, and said unto his master's wife, Behold, my master knoweth not what *is* with me in the house, and he hath committed all that he hath to my hand;
9 There is none greater in this house than I; neither hath he kept back anything from me but thee, because thou *art* his wife: how then can I do this great wickedness, and sin against God?
10 And it came to pass, as she spake to Joseph day by day, that he hearkened not unto her, to lie by her, *or* to be with her.
11 And it came to pass about this time that *Joseph* went into the house to do his business; and *there was* none of the men of the house there within.
12 And she caught him by his garment, saying, lie with me: and he left his garment in her hand, and fled, and got him out.
13 And it came to pass, when she saw that he had left his garment in her hand, and was fled forth,
14 That she called unto the men of her house, and spake unto them, saying, See, he hath brought in an Hebrew unto us to mock us; he came in unto me to lie with me, and I cried with a loud voice:
15 And it came to pass, when he heard that I lifted up my

voice and cried, that he left his garment with me, and fled, and got him out.

16 And she laid up his garment by her, until his lord came home.

17 And she spake unto him according to these words, saying, The Hebrew servant which thou hast brought unto us, came in unto me to mock me:

18 And it came to pass, as I lifted up my voice and cried that he left his garment with me, and fled out.

19 And it came to pass, when his master heard the words of his wife, which she spake unto him, saying after this manner did thy servant to me; that his wrath was kindled.

20 And Joseph's master took him, and put him into the prison, a place where the king's prisoners *were* bound: and he was there in the prison.

Rahab

Was she forced in prostitution living in Jericho? Possibly she was forced into this life style just to feed herself and her family, knowing full well that it would destroy her hopes of ever having a husband to give her children, to love and protect her. Her home was built into the city wall and was a good hideout because men were coming and going all the time. She obviously had some knowledge of God as she protected the spies with the hope of a better life for herself and her family.

The citizens of Jericho were well aware that several hundred thousand Israelites were camped only six miles to the east, across the Jordan River. The citizens were easily outnumbered. They had heard the stories of the God of the Israelites drying up the Red Sea and how the Israelites had already defeated two Amorite Kings. The officials of Jericho were desperately concerned. The city was thousands of years old. Jericho is the oldest city in the world, and at 670 feet below sea level, the lowest city in the world. In Rahab's day, several thousand people lived inside Jericho's strong walls.

Although located well off major trade routes and not an important city, the excavated tombs of Jericho's Kings indicate a well-developed culture.

The Israelites had been in the desert for approximately forty years, Moses had died and their new leader, Joshua, was ready to lead the people across the Jordan River to occupy the land. Before crossing the river, Joshua sent two spies to explore Jericho, the town they were approaching. Rahab had hidden the two spies under stalks of flax on the roof, she lied to the king. The King of Jericho had his own spies and told Rahab to turn over the two Hebrews. She said two men she did not know had come to her house and left just before dark. She deliberately lied as she told the king's men to look for the spies along the road between Jericho and the Jordan River. This woman of strong courage then proposed a deal to the spies. It was a deal based on her faith **"the Lord your God is God in heaven above and here on Earth. I know that the Lord has given you this land."** Did she acquire this knowledge of God from her Father, her Mother or Grandmother?

In return for saving the spies, Rahab asked them to save her and her family when they took the city. The spies agreed and told Rahab to get her family into her house and then to hang a scarlet cord from a window overlooking the city wall. The Israelite army would spare everyone in the house with the scarlet cord. Rahab then lowered a rope so the spies could escape over the wall, and told them to go into the hills away from the Jordan River, to give the king's men time to give up the hunt and return to Jericho.

The two spies reported back to Joshua. **"We are sure that the Lord has given us the whole country. All the people there are terrified of us."** They also told of the key role Rahab the prostitute had played.

According to Scripture, the Israelites crossed the Jordan River at harvest time when the river was flooded. As soon as the priests leading the thousands of people stepped into the river, "the water stopped flowing and piled up, far upstream." The Israelites walked across on dry land. When they got to Jericho, they quietly marched around Jericho once a day for six days. On the seventh day they marched around seven times, blew their trumpets, shouted and "the walls collapsed.

After the walls fell down and before Joshua burned Jericho, he instructed his men to take Rahab and her family to safety. And the Bible says, **"her descendants have lived in Israel to this day."**

Joshua 6:25;
25 And Joshua saved Rahab the harlot alive, and her father's household, and all that she had; and she dwelleth in Israel *even* unto this day; because she hid the messengers, which Joshua sent to spy out Jericho.

I believe that God honored her life and that she became a Proverbs 31 woman in spite of her past history because as I said, she and her descendants still live in Israel to this day.

Rahab is mentioned three times in the Renewed Testament. Matthew says she is an ancestor of Jesus. In both books of Hebrews, she is commended for her faith, and in James, she is commended for her good works. Did she become a Proverbs 31 Woman? Joshua 2:1-24, 6:16-25, Matthew 1:5, Hebrews 11:31, James 2:25.

Jericho was eventually rebuilt. Mark Anthony gave Jericho as a gift to Cleopatra. After their deaths, the city came under the control of Herod, who built a winter palace nearby.

Gomer
God instructed Hosea (a prophet) to marry a prostitute because the Children of Israel had committed prostitution by their idolatry to other gods. In the Old Testament book written by Hosea, the prostitute Gomer represents the unfaithful Children of Israel, and Hosea, a loving God. God

wanted to show the Children of Israel that he still loved them, no matter how unfaithful they were to Him. He is a God of restoration and redemption.

Sections of this story are uncomfortable because Hosea, who represents God as a prophet, sounds like an abusive husband. After Hosea and Gomer married they had two sons and a daughter. Hosea tells his three children to plead with their mother to stop her adultery and prostitution and detail how he will deal harshly with her: he will "strip her naked," build a wall to block her way," and "she will die of thirst." God speaks and says, **"I will punish her for the times that she forgot me, when she burned incense to Baal and put on her jewelry to go chasing after her lovers."** This has more to do with God's punishment of Israel for its sins and rebellious attitude than with Hosea's intentions for Gomer. Gomer had returned back to prostitution, selling herself to other men.

Hosea pursued her. In fact, he bought Gomer in a slave market and said to her, **"From now on you're living with me. No more whoring, no more sleeping around. You're living with me and I'm living with you."**

Hosea told Gomer that they would be faithful to each other. **"I will win her back with words of love. Then once again she will call me her husband."** Hosea forgave her (he reacted to her hurt) and redeemed her from the slave market in spite of his humiliation. Did he teach her Proverbs 31? It requires a rare man to love this type of woman. Did she begin to produce for her husband? Care for their children? Love working? Did she begin to schedule her work around the needs of other people? If so, did she become a Proverbs 31 woman according to Hosea's teaching and instruction with love and compassion? Obviously she thought she was not worthy of Hosea's embrace or his affection. I would like to believe that she began to monitor the conduct of herself and the behavior of her household in order that her husband could sit at the gate with pride abiding in Torah because God is a

God of redemption and restoration. And most of all: HER HUSBAND PRAISED HER!.

Only a few years after Hosea wrote this, Assyria invaded Israel and after a three year siege of its capital city, carried the people into captivity. The Scripture states over and over that this was/is punishment because of Israel's (people) unfaithfulness to God: they were like prostitutes. The Assyrian army was known to be ruthless and savage. They burned cities, chopped off people's hands, beheaded others and cut open the uterus of pregnant women.

For the very first time, God is pictured as a divine lover. God would pursue the nation Israel and restore it, just as Hosea pursued his faithless wife and brought her back home. God would give his people forgiveness, a second chance, a new beginning. **Hosea 1, 2, 3**

Delilah

She is described as being one of the lowest, meanest women of the Bible-used Samson, the strongest man in his world. Deceiving Samson was not her idea, though. She wanted money and she did it for money, a lot of money. But was she actually one of the lowest, meanest women of the Bible? She was superbly skilled in the art of seduction.

God put the Israelites under the domination of the Philistines for 40 years because of their disobedience and sin. The Philistines were a rough and tumble enemies of the Israelites and known for their week long drinking parties.

When Samson was born, his parents set him apart for God, meaning he was not to drink strong drink, touch a dead body or **cut his hair.** Samson was incredibly strong. At his wedding feast to his Philistine bride-to-be, he told his 30 Philistine groomsmen that he would give each one a change of fine clothing if they answered his riddle. Unable to answer it, they threatened to kill his bride if she failed to get the answer for them. She cried. She pouted. **"You don't love me! You told my friends a riddle and didn't tell me what**

it means!" Worn out by her nagging, Samson told her the secret, and she, of course, told the 30 Philistines. Samson got so upset, he killed 30 other Philistines, took their clothes and gave their clothes to the 30 at the wedding feast. The marriage did not take place, but as a result, a series of battles took place in which Samson killed more than 1,000 Philistines. Then, after leading Israel for 20 years, he went to the city of Hebron, where he met Delilah.

The Bible does not tell us much about Delilah except that Samson loved her. Was she beautiful? Did she know how to please him as a Proverbs 31 Woman would, to be a comfort, a counterpart, a completer? Once again the Bible does not say, but whatever her charms Samson was madly in love with her. Samson's weakness for women was well known when he fell in love with Delilah. He trusted her.

Delilah may have loved Samson also. That is until some Philistine leaders offered her a huge amount of money to seduce him and discover the source of his legendary strength. They wanted him in order to impregnate their women in order to have sons as strong as Samson. Delilah used all her feminine wiles, her skilled touch, her kisses, her ability to comfort, and then said, **"Tell me, dear, the secret of your great strength, and how you can be tied up and humbled."**

Samson did not easily give up his secrets, telling Delilah, **"If they were to tie me up with seven bowstrings, then I would become weak, just like anyone else."** So Delilah got fresh bowstrings and tied him up, but he broke them easily.

"Come now, Samson-you're playing with me. Be serious; tell me how you can be tied up."

Samson told her to bind him with brand new ropes and he would lose his strength. Then he told her that if she made seven braids in his hair and wove the seven braids into a fabric on a loom, he would be weak. Both times he was lying. One would think that Samson would have figured out that Delilah was up to no good, but, love is blind.

Then she used the same trump card his bride-to-be had used before. **"How can you say 'I love you' when you won't even trust me?"** Delilah nagged Samson until he told her that if his hair were to be cut, his strength would be gone. She knew he was telling the truth this time.

After getting paid by the Philistine leaders, she put Samson to sleep and a Philistine barber cut off Samson's locks. When he awoke, his strength was gone; God had abandoned him because he had broken his oath. Please know that his strength was NOT in his hair. The Philistines captured Samson, gouged out his eyes, bound him in fetters and took him to a prison. Eventually he was brought to a temple of one of their gods. There he prayed for forgiveness and strength and pulled down the pillars of the temple, killing many Philistines as he died, "so the dead whom he slew at his death were more than those whom he had slain during his life. **Judges 16:30**
We do not know anything more about Delilah, the woman who loved money and knew how to manipulate the strongest man in the world with the simple words, **"If you really loved me...."** A Proverbs 31 woman does not nag. Her lips were not sweet, her words were not smooth. The grave was in her mouth and caused a wound in the heart. She danced down a primrose path and took Samson with her. Had she been a Proverbs 31 woman, her mouth with kindness would flow. Her words would never destroy, she would not tear down. Her words would never paralyze, instead her words would have brought life, and hope and would have restored. She would not have been easily deceived with money or desired such. Her seeds of kindness would have produced the desired harvest and perhaps she and Samson would have lived happily together, but of course that did not happen. Her greed destroyed not only her but Samson. Sadly, she knew NOT Torah nor the God of Abraham, Isaac or Jacob.

Solomon describes Delilah in Proverbs which seems to

be a perfect description:

> The lips of a seductive woman are oh so sweet,
> her soft words are oh so smooth.
> But it won't be long before she's grave 1 in your mouth,
> a pain in your gut, a wound in your heart.
> She's dancing down the primrose path to death;
> she's headed straight for hell and taking you with her.

Jezebel

She was the daughter of the king of Tyre and she worshipped Baal, "Ruler of the Universe: and one of the pagan gods of Phoenica. Jezebel did not just worship Baal, she was a fanatic. She believed that Baal was the ruler of the universe, lord of war and source of life and fertility. When she moved from Tyre to Ahab's magnificent ivory palace, she took with her 450 priests of Baal and 400 prophets of Asherah, a goddess the Bible called "a sacred whore." Israel's official religion was not exciting enough for Jezebel. Baal ceremonies included burning children alive while the worshippers took part in sex orgies so the gods would grant a bountiful harvest and increased fertility. It is no wonder that God told the children of Israel to have nothing to do with Baal, but they refused to listen.

After the death of Solomon, the nation was divided into the Northern kingdom, called Israel, and the Southern kingdom, called Judah. When Omri, the sixth King of the Northern kingdom, wanted to strengthen his alliance with Tyre, his son, Prince Ahab, marry Princess Jezebel.

Ahab encouraged the worship of Baal because he did whatever Jezebel told him to do. He built a temple to Baal next to his palace. Ahab did more to arouse the anger of the Lord than all the previous kings of Israel combined. When the prophets of the Lord opposed Baal worship, Jezebel ordered them killed. Jezebel apparently had no wisdom, no trust in the God of Abraham, Isaac or Jacob. She outwardly had no morals. She was lazy and desired riches. Did she have obedience to her parents, maybe yes, maybe no. They worshiped a pagan god, Baal and apparently taught her to do so. She loathed and despised anything that was not like Baal. Had she been a Proverbs 31 woman she would have produced for her man what his money could not produce for himself. She would have understood the needs of her King and husband. She would have responded to the hurts of others rather than plan death of children and had orgies (parties). She would have loved God with all her strength, but sadly she died a horrible death, thrown from a window and dogs ate her as Elijah (prophet) predicted.

Ahab should have NEVER built a temple to Baal for her or went along with the death of Naboth. He did NOT in any way assume his responsibility for his Kingdom (people) let alone his wife. It could have been otherwise and Ahab could have experienced the closest thing to Heaven a man will ever experience on earth, the Love of Jezebel.

Ahab wanted to buy a vineyard next to his palace, but the owner, Naboth, refused to sell it, citing Israel's law that property should be handed down through a family. The Bible says that Ahab was so upset, **"he went to bed, stuffed his face in his pillow and refused to eat."** This reaction was not one anyone would expect from a powerful king who had conquered nations.

Jezebel confronted him" **"Well, are you the king or aren't you? Get out of bed, cheer up, and eat. I will get you Naboth's vineyard!"** So Jezebel set to work arranging Naboth's death.

Using Ahab's seal instead of her own, she wrote a letter telling the elders in Naboth's city, having him falsely accused of blaspheming God and the King. As a result Naboth and his family were thrown into the street, stoned and killed. Jezebel then told Ahab to go get the vineyard.

Jezebel suffered a tragic death. Years later, Jehu killed King Jehoram of Israel and went to the capital city to be crowned King himself. Hearing that Jehu had arrived, Jezebel put on makeup, fixed her hair, posed seductively at her window and called down to Jehu, taunting him, **"So, how are things, you dashing King-killer?"**

Jehu ordered some men to throw her out of the window. She died on the pavement, trampled under the hooves of Jehu's horses.

Later that day, Jehu gave orders to bury Jezebel's body: **"Take that cursed woman and bury her; after all, she is a King's daughter."** But his servants found that dogs had eaten her, leaving only her skull, feet and hands; just as the prophet Elijah had predicted. 1 Kings 16:31-32; 18:1-19; 19:1-3; 21:1-29; 11 Kings 9:30-37

Herodias and Salome

Herodias came from a family with a long history of brutality, viciousness, murder, and self-interest. Herodias became an orphan when her Grandfather, Herod the Great, executed her Father and Grandmother. He then arranged for Herodias to marry her half uncle, Herod Philip, and they had one child, a daughter Salome. The question is: What would make a woman use her own daughter to seduce her husband so that he would kill a man?

When Salome was about 10 years old, she and her parents were living in Rome. When Herod Antipas, half uncle of Herodias and half brother of Philip, visited them, Herodias and Antipas began an affair. The infatuated Antipas divorced his wife, and Herodias left Philip to marry Antipas. They moved back to Israel, where he was ruler of Galilee and Perea.

Under Jewish law, a man was forbidden to marry his brother's divorced wife. John the Baptist was not shy about pointing this out, proclaiming that Herodias and Antipas were living in adultery. Antipas was convinced that John the Baptist was a holy man, so he was afraid of public reaction if he executed him. However, Herodias was "smoldering with hate," and nagged Antipas until he finally put John the Baptist in prison.

Shortly afterwards, Antipas gave a lavish birthday party for himself at Machaerus, a magnificent fortress and Herodians pleasure palace on the Eastern side of the Dead Sea. While John the Baptist was imprisoned in a cell in Machaerus, the many male guests ate and drank plentifully, reclining on cushioned couches around long banquet tables. Musicians played and the women dancers entertained.

Late in the night when the guests were drunk and Antipas, himself was also quite intoxicated, he called for Salome, his voluptuous young stepdaughter, to dance. Salome danced seductively, removing her seven veils one by one while revealing more and more of her slowly gyrating body. Antipas was so pleased he said, **"I will give you anything you want...I swear that I will give you even as much as half my kingdom!"** Antipas was not thinking clearly due to intoxication.

Herodias took advantage of this opportunity. She had probably coached Salome how to dance and what to say, **"I want you to give me here and now the head of John the Baptist on a plate!"** She was not a Proverbs 31 woman. She energized her daughter to evil, she decided because of her hatred for John the Baptist to have his head cut off (murder), and she used her daughter to accomplish this evil act. She persuaded, and she convinced, so the dance of the seven veils began and ended with murder. She was not Torah observant and had no compassion. She had no feelings but of hatred. She did not shield herself from damaged people. She was involved in her own wants, needs and desires. She could and she would have her own way no matter the outcome.

Antipas had no desire to kill John the Baptist, but he did not want to lose face with his so called friends. He ordered the executioner to bring him John's head on a platter. He presented it to Salome, who gave it to her mother. When Jesus disciples heard about his death, they came and got his body and buried it in a tomb.

The Scriptures tell us little more about Herodias, although it does say that Pilate sent Jesus to Antipas when he learned that Jesus was a Galilean. Antipas had wanted to meet Jesus and asked him many questions, but Jesus refused to answer him. Antipas turned on Jesus, mocked him, dressed him in a King costume and sent him back to Pilate.

Antipas was stripped of his position by the Roman Emperor and banished to Gaul. Although she could have had her freedom, Herodias chose to go with her husband into exile. It is said that they both died in Spain.

Matthew 14:1-12
1 At that time Herod the tetrarch heard of the fame of Jesus,
2 And said unto his servants, this is John the Baptist; he is risen from the dead; and therefore mighty works do shew forth themselves in him.
3 For Herod had laid hold on John, and bound him, and put *him* in prison for Herodias' sake and his brother Philip's wife.
4 For John said unto him, It is not lawful for thee to have her.
5 And when he would have put him to death, he feared the multitude, because they counted him as a prophet.
6 But when Herod's birthday was kept, the daughter of Herodias danced before them, and pleased Herod.
7 Whereupon he promised with an oath to give her whatsoever she would ask.
8 And she, being before instructed of her mother, said, Give me here John Baptist's head in a charger.
9 And the king was sorry: nevertheless for the oath's sake, and them which sat with him at meat, he commanded *it* to be given *her*.
10 And he sent, and beheaded John in the prison.
11 And his head was brought in a charger, and given to the damsel: and she brought *it* to her mother.
12 And his disciples came, and took up the body, and buried

it, and went and told Jesus.

Mark 6:14-29

14 And king Herod heard *of him*; (for his name was spread abroad:) and he said, That John the Baptist was risen from the dead, and therefore mighty works do shew forth themselves in him.

15 Others said that it is Elias. And others said, that it is a prophet, or as one of the prophets.

16 But when Herod heard *thereof*, he said, It is John, whom I beheaded: he is risen from the dead.

17 For Herod himself had sent forth and laid hold upon John, and bound him in prison for Herodias' sake, his brother Philip's wife: for he had married her.

18 For John had said unto Herod, It is not lawful for thee to have thy brother's wife.

19 Therefore Herodias had a quarrel against him, and would have killed him; but she could not:

20 For Herod feared John, knowing that he was a just man and an holy, and observed him; and when he heard him, he did many things, and heard him gladly.

21 And when a convenient day was come, that Herod on his birthday made a supper to his lords, high captains, and chief *estates* of Galilee;

22 And when the daughter of the said Herodias came in, and danced, and pleased Herod and them that sat with him, the king said unto the damsel, Ask of me whatsoever thou wilt, and I will give *it* thee.

23 And he sware unto her, Whatsoever thou shalt ask of me, I will give *it* thee, unto the half of my kingdom.

24 And she went forth, and said unto her mother, What shall I ask? And she said, The head of John the Baptist.

25 And she came in straightway with haste unto the king, and asked, saying, I will that thou give me by and by in a charger the head of John the Baptist.

26 And the king was exceeding sorry; *yet* for his oath's sake,

and for their sakes which sat with him, he would not reject her.
27 And immediately the king sent an executioner, and commanded his head to be brought: and he went and beheaded him in the prison,
28 And brought his head in a charger, and gave it to the damsel: and the damsel gave it to her mother.
29 And when his disciples heard *of it*, they came and took up his corpse, and laid it in a tomb.

Cunning and Deceptive Women

Rebekah

She did not appear to be "one of the lowest and meanest women" like Delilah. She was not "the wickedest woman in the world" like Jezebel. She was not guilty of causing a vicious murder like Herodias, nevertheless, despite her good qualities, Rebekah was one of the most cunning and deceptive women of the Bible or was she?

After Sarah died, Abraham did not want his son, Isaac, to marry a Canaanite woman. He sent his servant to Haran, where Abraham's brother lived, to find a wife for Isaac. When the servant arrived in Haran, he stopped at the town's well and prayed God to show him the right woman, a woman who, when he asked for water, would also offer to get water for his 10 camels. Watering camel's by women was unheard of for camel's dislike women extremely. Before the servant prayer was finished, Rebekah walked up, got water for the servant and said, **"I will also bring water for your camels and let them have all they want."** Wow!

Rebekah was the Granddaughter of Abraham's brother, stunningly beautiful and a virgin. She was vivacious, friendly, outgoing, unselfish and energetic. Rebekah's family agreed that she should marry Isaac and sent her to him with their blessing so that she should become "the mother of thousand of ten thousands." Rebekah became Isaac's wife "and he loved her."

Twenty years after their marriage, she became pregnant with twins. They tumbled and kicked so much in her womb that she asked God what was going on. God told her, **"Two nations are within you; you will give birth to two rival peoples. One will be stronger than the other; the older will serve the younger."** Esau, the older, was a boisterous hunter and outdoorsman and favored by Isaac. Jacob, the younger, was more clever and thoughtful than his brother, preferred a quiet life indoors, and was favored by Rebekah.

As the oldest, it was Esau's right to inherit most of his Father's property and to become the family patriarch. But in an amazingly shortsighted moment, Esau gave his birthright, his ancestral heritage, to Jacob in exchange for some bread and a bowl of lentil stew. The story is told that Esau had just killed Nimod and his security guard and that he was running for his life, at which time, he obtained food from his brother, Jacob. This was an exchange between the two brothers.

In addition to the birthright, the oldest son would receive his Father's blessing, the right to become the head of the family after Isaac's death. The giving of a blessing was a serious business and once given, it could not be revoked or taken back.

Isaac had become blind. Rebekah was eavesdropping when Isaac told Esau to fix a meal of wild game for him and he would bless Esau. Isaac was very fond of wild game. As soon as Esau went hunting, Rebekah told Jacob how they would trick/deceive Isaac into giving the blessing meant for Esau to Jacob. She would cook two goats to taste like wild game and put goatskins on Jacob's hands and neck so he would feel hairy like Esau. Jacob would wear Esau's clothes so he would smell like his brother.

Jacob worried that if Isaac realized he was being deceived that he would curse Jacob instead of bless him. **"Let any curse against you fall on me, my son,"** she said. **"Just do as I say, and go and get the goats for me."** She was very serious about this deception and Jacob followed her instructions.

The deception worked and Isaac blessed Jacob. As soon as Jacob walked out of Isaac's tent, Esau arrived with the dinner he had prepared. "Who are you?" asked Isaac, thinking that Esau had just left. All at once, Isaac and Esau realized that they had been duped. Isaac trembled and shook. Esau cried out loudly and bitterly, and threatened to kill his brother.

Rebekah sent Jacob to Haran to find a wife. The real reason for Jacob to leave was so that his brother could not kill him. As Rebekah watched Jacob start off on his long journey, she probably did not realize that she would never see her beloved son again.

Rebekah died before Jacob returned, all the time living with a husband who had been deceived by her and a son who resented her for stealing his blessing. She was buried in the same cave in Hebron as Abraham and Sarah (where Isaac would be buried a few years later).

Proverbs 31:11 says **"The heart of her husband doth safely trust in her, so that he shall have no need of spoil." Everyone trusts somebody somewhere, at some time. Do not betray the confidence of another. Every man trust his woman. But does the woman trust her man. Isaac taught Rebekah how to be deceitful and she turned the tables on him with Jacob. Did Isaac know that he could trust her with his weaknesses'. Could he trust her with his money or jewel's. Could he trust her with his secrets or trust her with his memories. Could he trust her to be faithful around his friends? We do not know the answer to these questions, but we do know that a Proverbs 31 woman will give her man what his achievements cannot give him. She will do him good and not evil all the days of her life. Or will she as with Jacob?**

The prophecy given to Rebekah many years earlier about her twin sons came true. Esau became the Father of the

Edomites, a people who lived south of the Dead Sea and were an enemy of the Israelites. Jacob, whose name was changed to Israel after fighting with an angel, became the Father of the Jews, who are also known as the Children of Israel. Genesis 24:1-67, 25:19-34, 27:1 – 28:5.

Tamar, Daughter-in-law Of Judah

Was she cunning? To make sense of the bizarre and uncomfortable story of Tamar, it is necessary to understand the custom of levirate marriage. (Levirate means "husband's brother).

If a man dies without children and his wife is of childbearing age, the man's brother is obligated to marry the man's widow and take care of her. Their first son becomes the heir of the dead man. This custom has been practiced in China, India and countries in Africa and the Pacific. It was widespread in the ancient world, including among the Canaanites and the Israelites.

A levirate marriage provides for the welfare of the widow in a patriarchal society. Without it, she could become homeless and poverty stricken. It also provides a way to pass the dead man's property to his wife and daughters because, without a son, property might be divided among the man's male relatives.

Judah, son of Leah and Jacob married a Canaanite woman, even though his Grandfather, Abraham had told his Father, Jacob, "Don't marry a Canaanite."

Judah and his wife had three sons: Er, Onan and Shelah. Er, the oldest married Tamar, who probably was also a Canaanite. The Scriptures say that Er's conduct was so evil that God killed him before he and Tamar had children.

Judah told Onan, his second son, **"Go and sleep with your brother's widow. Fulfill your obligation to her as her husband's brother, so that your brother may have descendants."** Rather than heeding his Father's wishes, Onan exploited Tamar by taking advantage of her sexually but destroying his semen, letting it spill on the ground. He knew any children would be Er's, not his. This selfishness displeased God and he killed Onan as well.

Judah had lost two of his three sons and was concerned about losing Shelah too. Using the excuse that Shelah was too young to marry, he told Tamar to go home to her Father's house. The Proverbs 31 woman knows her man's needs may change in a single second. She moves. She changes to meet the circumstances. She is ready for change like the ship that moves from port to port. God loves variation. A cat loves to be rubbed. A dog loves to be patted. Birds love to fly and ducks and geese like to honk and quack. Tamar was incredibly flexible. She dressed the part. It took time, she was not waiting for the opportunity to present itself. She had a strong sense of purpose or focus on her assignment, to have a baby regardless of Judah. She had a plan. That is a Proverbs 31 woman. No whining about her home life. No griping or yelling was considered. Her needs necessitated change and she got it. Proverbs 31:25 says "Strength and honor are her clothing and she shall rejoice in time to come." She gave birth to Judah's child and he declared her more righteous than he.

Judah and his sons are not pictured as a very likable bunch. Er was evil. Clearly Onan wronged Tamar. And Judah wronged her when he sent her back to her Father's house instead of taking care of her himself. In a society where women relied on their husbands for their security and their value was in bearing children, Tamar had been mistreated and rejected. She seemed to be powerless.

But when Judah's wife died, Tamar took control of her own destiny and the destiny of Judah's line. She dressed like a temple prostitute and sat by the side of the road where she knew Judah would travel. Judah approached her and asked how much she would charge to have sex with him.

Tamar was clever, cunning and a good negotiator. Rather than name a price, she asked what Judah would give her for her services. He offered a young goat, which he would bring to her later. To ensure he would come back, she asked him to give her his seal with its cord and his walking stick. The transaction was completed. Each side gave what the other wanted. When Judah left, Tamar changed her clothes and went home with the seal and stick Judah had given her. And Tamar was pregnant.

Three months later, when Tamar's pregnancy was showing, Judah became incensed that his daughter-in-law had been acting like a whore and ordered that she be killed. **"I am pregnant by the man who owns these things,"** she said, showing him his own seal and walking stick.

Judah, who had horribly wronged Tamar and, in self-righteousness, was about to have her killed, did a complete turn around: **"She is more righteous than I, since I did not give her to my son Shelah."**

This courageous, wise, clever woman took matters in her own hands, after repeatedly being wronged by Judah and his sons (evil and lustful men who thought they could do whatever they wanted with her and then send her home as damaged goods). She took a huge risk to see justice done and protect her family rights.

Tamar gave birth to twin boys, Perez and Zerah. Although she had children, she most likely never had a second husband. However, because of Tamar's "righteous" action, Judah's father, Jacob, could, on his deathbed, praise Judah and promise that "his descendants will always rule." Judah and Tamar's son Perez was the ancestor of David, Israel's greatest king and the ancestor of Jesus Christ, the King of Kings.

Genesis 38:1-30
1 And it came to pass at that time, that Judah went down from his brethren, and turned in to a certain Adullamite, whose name *was* Hirah.
2 And Judah saw there a daughter of a certain Canaanite,

whose name *was* Shuah; and he took her, and went in unto her.

3 And she conceived, and bare a son; and he called his name Er.

4 And she conceived again, and bare a son; and she called his name Onan.

5 And she yet again conceived, and bare a son; and called his name Shelah: and he was at Chezib, when she bare him.

6 And Judah took a wife for Er his firstborn, whose name *was* Tamar.

7 And Er, Judah's firstborn, was wicked in the sight of the LORD; and the LORD slew him.

8 And Judah said unto Onan, Go in unto thy brother's wife, and marry her, and raise up seed to thy brother.

9 And Onan knew that the seed should not be his; and it came to pass, when he went in unto his brother's wife, that he spilled *it* on the ground, lest that he should give seed to his brother.

10 And the thing which he did displeased the LORD: wherefore he slew him also.

11 Then said Judah to Tamar his daughter in law, Remain a widow at thy father's house, till Shelah my son be grown: for he said, Lest peradventure he die also, as his brethren *did*. And Tamar went and dwelt in her father's house.

12 And in process of time the daughter of Shuah Judah's wife died; and Judah was comforted, and went up unto his sheepshearers to Timnath, he and his friend Hirah the Adullamite.

13 And it was told Tamar, saying, Behold thy father in law goeth up to Timnath to shear his sheep.

14 And she put her widow's garments off from her, and covered her with a veil, and wrapped herself, and sat in an open place, which *is* by the way to Timnath; for she saw that Shelah was grown, and she was not given unto him to wife.

15 When Judah saw her, he thought her *to be* an harlot; because she had covered her face.

16 And he turned unto her by the way, and said, Go to, I pray thee, let me come in unto thee; (for he knew not that she *was* his daughter in law.) And she said, what wilt thou give me, that thou mayest come in unto me?

17 And he said, I will send *thee* a kid from the flock. And she said, Wilt thou give *me* a pledge, till thou send *it*?

18 And he said, what pledge shall I give thee? And she said, Thy signet, and thy bracelets, and thy staff that *is* in thine hand. And he gave *it* her, and came in unto her, and she conceived by him.

19 And she arose, and went away, and laid her veil from her, and put on the garments of her widowhood.

20 And Judah sent the kid by the hand of his friend the Adulamite, to receive *his* pledge from the woman's hand: but he found her not.

21 Then he asked the men of that place, saying, where *is* the harlot, that *was* openly by the way side? And they said, There was no harlot in this *place*.

22 And he returned to Judah, and said, I cannot find her; and also the men of the place said, *that* there was no harlot in this *place*.

23 And Judah said, Let her take *it* to her, lest we be shamed: behold, I sent this kid, and thou hast not found her.

24 And it came to pass about three months after, that it was told Judah, saying, Tamar thy daughter in law hath played the harlot; and also, behold, she *is* with child by whoredom. And Judah said, bring her forth, and let her be burnt.

25 When she *was* brought forth, she sent to her father in law, saying, By the man, whose these *are, am* I with child: and she said, Discern, I pray thee, whose *are* these, the signet, and bracelets, and staff.

26 And Judah acknowledged *them*, and said, She hath been more righteous than I; because that I gave her not to Shelah my son. And he knew her again no more.

27 And it came to pass in the time of her travail, that, behold, twins *were* in her womb.

28 And it came to pass, when she travailed, that *the one* put out *his* hand: and the midwife took and bound upon his hand a scarlet thread, saying, This came out first.
29 And it came to pass, as he drew back his hand, that, behold, his brother came out: and she said, How hast thou broken forth? *this* breach *be* upon thee: therefore his name was called Pharez.
30 And afterward came out his brother, that had the scarlet thread upon his hand: and his name was called Zarah.

Women Of Jeremiah 44 Were Not Proverbs 31 Women

The following women were obviously not Proverbs 31 woman.

Jeremiah 44:15-27
15 Then all the men which knew that their wives had burned incense unto other gods, and all the women that stood by, a great multitude, even all the people that dwelt in the land of Egypt, in Pathros, answered Jeremiah, saying,
16 *As for* the word that thou hast spoken unto us in the name of the LORD, we will not hearken unto thee.
17 But we will certainly do whatsoever thing goeth forth out of our own mouth, to burn incense unto the queen of heaven, and to pour out drink offerings unto her, as we have done, we, and our fathers, our kings, and our princes, in the cities of Judah, and in the streets of Jerusalem: for *then* had we plenty of victuals, and were well, and saw no evil.
18 But since we left off to burn incense to the queen of heaven, and to pour out drink offerings unto her, we have wanted all *things*, and have been consumed by the sword and by the famine.
19 And when we burned incense to the queen of heaven, and poured out drink offerings unto her, did we make her cakes to worship her, and pour out drink offerings unto her, without our men?

20 Then Jeremiah said unto all the people, to the men, and to the women, and to all the people which had given him *that* answer, saying,
21 The incense that ye burned in the cities of Judah, and in the streets of Jerusalem, ye, and your fathers, your kings, and your princes, and the people of the land, did not the LORD remember them, and came it *not* into his mind?
22 So that the LORD could no longer bear, because of the evil of your doings, *and* because of the abominations which ye have committed; therefore is your land a desolation, and an astonishment, and a curse, without an inhabitant, as at this day.
23 Because ye have burned incense, and because ye have sinned against the LORD, and have not obeyed the voice of the LORD, nor walked in his law, nor in his statutes, nor in his testimonies; therefore this evil is happened unto you, as at this day.
24 Moreover Jeremiah said unto all the people, and to all the women, Hear the word of the LORD, all Judah that *are* in the land of Egypt:
25 Thus saith the LORD of hosts, the God of Israel, saying; Ye and your wives have both spoken with your mouths, and fulfilled with your hand, saying, We will surely perform our vows that we have vowed, to burn incense to the queen of heaven, and to pour out drink offerings unto her: ye will surely accomplish your vows, and surely perform your vows.
26 Therefore hear ye the word of the LORD, all Judah that dwell in the land of Egypt; Behold, I have sworn by my great name, saith the LORD, that my name shall no more be named in the mouth of any man of Judah in all the land of Egypt, saying, The Lord GOD liveth.
27 Behold, I will watch over them for evil, and not for good: and all the men of Judah that *are* in the land of Egypt shall be consumed by the sword and by the famine, until there be an end of them.

Beautiful Women Of The Bible

The five most beautiful women in the world were said to be Abigail, Rahab, Esther, Sarah and Rebekah. According to Jewish culture these women had a "double beauty", beautiful when young and also a beauty even in old age.

Although Proverbs says, "Charm is deceitful, and beauty is vain, but a woman who fears the Lord is to be praised," there are a number of other women of the Bible who are noted for their beauty: Eve, Rebekah, Rachel, Bathsheba, Tamar (the daughter of David), Abishag, and the daughters of Job.

There are no pictures, of course, and different cultures have different opinions of beauty. The closest we can get to an image of what men considered beautiful in the days of King Solomon is from the Song of Solomon, in which a man describes his bride:

> *How beautiful are your feet in sandals,*
> *O noble daughter!*
> *Your rounded thighs are like jewels,*
> *the work of a master hand.*
> *Your navel is a rounded bowl*
> *that never lacks mixed wine,*
> *Your belly is a heap of wheat,*
> *encircled with lilies.*
> *Your two breasts are like two fawns,*
> *twins of a gazelle.*
> *Your neck is like an ivory tower.*
> *Your eyes are pools in Heshbon,*
> *by the gates of Bath-rabbim.*
> *Your nose is like a tower of Lebanon,*
> *which looks toward Damascus.*
> *Your head crowns you like Carmel,*
> *and your flowing locks are like purple;*
> *a king is held captive in the tresses.*

--
How beautiful and pleasant you are,
O loved one, with all your delights!
Your stature is like a palm tree,
and your breasts are like its clusters.
I say I will climb the palm tree,
and lay hold of its fruit.
Oh may your breasts be like clusters of the vine,
and the scent of your breath like apples,
and your mouth like the best wine.

Abigail

She was an astute, diplomatic and intelligent woman with a dazzlingly beautiful body. She was married to a rich, drunken jerk, Nabal, a wealthy sheep rancher described as a "mean, ill-tempered man," whom owned 3,000 sheep and 1,000 goats. He was boorish, uncouth and ill-mannered. Nabal and Abigail had an impressive home where Abigail hosted large and long celebrations with much food and drink during sheep-shearing season, a time of eating, drinking and partying in ancient Israel.

Because David's right to the throne was being contested by the existing King Saul; David and 600 men of his followers were hiding out in the wilderness near where Nabal and Abigail lived. David sent 20 of his men to Nabal, who greeted him with peace and told Nabal they had protected his sheep and workers. David's men needed food and asked Nabal to be generous and share the feast Abigail and her servants had prepared. Since David had protected Nabal's property, the request was a legitimate one.

With much bravado, Nabal insulted David's men. **"David? Who is he? I've never heard of him!"**

David did not take Nabal's slap in the face kindly and ordered 400 of his men to take up their swords and set out for Nabal's house.

Meanwhile, a servant told Abigail what had happened.

Being a Proverbs 31 woman she immediately packed 200 loaves of bread, five dressed sheep, two skins of wine and more food onto donkeys. When she found David, she fell on her knees before him: **My master, let me take the blame! Don't dwell on what that brute Nabal did... take this gift that I, your servant girl, have brought to my master, and give it to the young men."** Abigail understood Nabal's business and that is why she could feed several hundred men in a single day without being advised weeks ahead of time. The average woman does not have a real grasp of her husband's flow of business. She does not understand the decision making. She does not even understand why he is weary at the end of the day and needs great creature comforts from his woman. A Proverbs 31 woman will learn the language of his business or work. She understands the laws of increase, problem solving and she is well versed in policies and procedures. When she came to David with the provisions, she did not waiver in unbelief, she was very humble, bowing before him and in faith, giving glory to God.

She took responsibility for her husband's insults and approached David with humility and diplomacy showing that she was a Proverbs 31 Woman.

Enamored by her beauty, her courage and the wisdom of her words, David called off his attack. **"Blessed be God, the God of Israel. He sent you to meet me! And blessed be your good sense! Bless you for keeping me from murder... If you had not come as quickly as you did, stopping me in my tracks, by morning there would have been nothing left of Nabal but dead meat."**

Abigail went home, where she found Nabal very drunk. When she told him the next morning what she had done to save his life, Nabal had a heart attack. He died 10 days later.

When David heard of Nabal's death, he asked Abigail to marry him. Abigail was a rich **aristocrat**, and yet her humility was amazing: **"I'm your servant, ready to do** anything you want. I'll even wash the feet of my master's servants!" She was rewarded for her courage and reverence for David's position. **She was cautious but also did not require reassurance from others for her behavior of generosity. She was a servant as well as a beautiful woman.**

We know that she had a son by David, but we are told almost nothing else about her. Abigail was the perfect wife for David, because while he was quick to act and tempestuous, she was humble, wise and diplomatic.

She was described as having wisdom from above. Her wisdom was also peaceful, gentle, and friendly; it is full of compassion and produces a harvest of good deeds; it is free from prejudice and hypocrisy."

1 Samuel 25:2-42

2 A certain man in Maon, who had property there at Carmel, was very wealthy. He had a thousand goats and three thousand sheep, which he was shearing in Carmel.

3 His name was Nabal and his wife's name was Abigail. She was an intelligent and beautiful woman, but her husband was surly and mean in his dealings—he was a Calebite.

4 While David was in the wilderness, he heard that Nabal was shearing sheep.

5 So he sent ten young men and said to them, "Go up to Nabal at Carmel and greet him in my name.

6 Say to him: 'Long life to you! Good health to you and your household! And good health to all that is yours!

7 " 'Now I hear that it is sheep-shearing time. When your shepherds were with us, we did not mistreat them, and the whole time they were at Carmel nothing of theirs was missing.

8 Ask your own servants and they will tell you. Therefore be favorable toward my men, since we come at a festive time. Please give your servants and your son David whatever you can find for them.' "

9 When David's men arrived, they gave Nabal this message in David's name. Then they waited.
10 Nabal answered David's servants, "Who is this David? Who is this son of Jesse? Many servants are breaking away from their masters these days.
11 Why should I take my bread and water, and the meat I have slaughtered for my shearers, and give it to men coming from who knows where?"
12 David's men turned around and went back. When they arrived, they reported every word.
13 David said to his men, "Each of you strap on your sword!" So they did, and David strapped his on as well. About four hundred men went up with David, while two hundred stayed with the supplies.
14 One of the servants told Abigail, Nabal's wife, "David sent messengers from the wilderness to give our master his greetings, but he hurled insults at them.
15 Yet these men were very good to us. They did not mistreat us, and the whole time we were out in the fields near them nothing was missing.
16 Night and day there was a wall around us the whole time we were herding our sheep near them.
17 Now think it over and see what you can do, because disaster is hanging over our master and his whole household. He is such a wicked man that no one can talk to him."
18 Abigail acted quickly. She took two hundred loaves of bread, two skins of wine, five dressed sheep, five sheaths of roasted grain, a hundred cakes of raisins and two hundred cakes of pressed figs, and loaded them on donkeys.
19 Then she told her servants, "Go on ahead; I'll follow you." But she did not tell her husband Nabal.
20 As she came riding her donkey into a mountain ravine, there were David and his men descending toward her, and she met them.
21 David had just said, "It's been useless—all my watching over this fellow's property in the wilderness so that nothing

of his was missing. He has paid me back evil for good.

22 May God deal with David, be it ever so severely, if by morning I leave alive one male of all who belong to him!"

23 When Abigail saw David, she quickly got off her donkey and bowed down before David with her face to the ground.

24 She fell at his feet and said: "Pardon your servant, my lord, and let me speak to you; hear what your servant has to say.

25 Please pay no attention, my lord, to that wicked man Nabal. He is just like his name—his name means Fool, and folly goes with him. And as for me, your servant, I did not see the men my lord sent.

26 And now, my lord, as surely as the Lord your God lives and as you live, since the Lord has kept you from bloodshed and from avenging yourself with your own hands, may your enemies and all who are intent on harming my lord be like Nabal.

27 And let this gift, which your servant has brought to my lord, be given to the men who follow you.

28 "Please forgive your servant's presumption. The Lord your God will certainly make a lasting dynasty for my lord, because you fight the Lord's battles, and no wrongdoing will be found in you as long as you live.

29 Even though someone is pursuing you to take your life, the life of my lord will be bound securely in the bundle of the living by the Lord your God, but the lives of your enemies he will hurl away as from the pocket of a sling.

30 When the Lord has fulfilled for my lord every good thing he promised concerning him and has appointed him ruler over Israel,

31 my lord will not have on his conscience the staggering burden of needless bloodshed or of having avenged himself. And when the Lord your God has brought my lord success, remember your servant."

32 David said to Abigail, "Praise be to the Lord, the God of Israel, who has sent you today to meet me.

33 May you be blessed for your good judgment and for keeping me from bloodshed this day and from avenging myself with my own hands.
34 Otherwise, as surely as the Lord, the God of Israel, lives, who has kept me from harming you, if you had not come quickly to meet me, not one male belonging to Nabal would have been left alive by daybreak."
35 Then David accepted from her hand what she had brought him and said, "Go home in peace. I have heard your words and granted your request."
36 When Abigail went to Nabal, he was in the house holding a banquet like that of a king. He was in high spirits and very drunk. So she told him nothing at all until daybreak.
37 Then in the morning, when Nabal was sober, his wife told him all these things, and his heart failed him and he became like a stone.
38 About ten days later, the Lord struck Nabal and he died.
39 When David heard that Nabal was dead, he said, "Praise be to the Lord, who has upheld my cause against Nabal for treating me with contempt. He has kept his servant from doing wrong and has brought Nabal's wrongdoing down on his own head." Then David sent word to Abigail, asking her to become his wife.
40 His servants went to Carmel and said to Abigail, "David has sent us to you to take you to become his wife."
41 She bowed down with her face to the ground and said, "I am your servant and am ready to serve you and wash the feet of my lord's servants."
42 Abigail quickly got on a donkey and, attended by her five female servants, went with David's messengers and became his wife.

Rahab
   She was a woman of strong courage and it is believed that she was beautiful. She is descried under "Women whom are not Proverbs 31 woman." or was she? She was not

indifferent to the needs of the spies that needed protection and they trusted in her. She demonstrated impeccable loyalty to the Israelites and was rewarded for such.

Esther

She is one of the true heroines of the Bible. Like Deborah, Esther was a woman of great strength and courage, but Esther is far better known. Deborah was not any less devout, any less courageous, any less diplomatic or any less wise. It is just that Esther had better press.

Deborah's entire story is told in one chapter of the Bible and then celebrated with a poem in the next. Esther's is told in a beautifully written 10-chapter book in the Old Testament. At the end of Esther's story, the Jews decide that "every Jewish family of every future generation" would "remember and observe the days of Purim for all time to come." And so more than 2,500 years later, one month before Passover, Jews all over the world celebrate Esther's role in saving her people from genocide by anti-Semitic Persians. Each Purim in their synagogues, Jews perform a short, light-hearted play called a "Purim spiel," in which the story of Esther's heroics is depicted. The actors are often children, and the congregation participates by hissing and booing and rattling noisemakers every time Haman's name is mentioned.

In the third year of his 27-year reign as the most powerful King in the world, Ahasuerus had a six-month celebration to show off the splendor of his imperial court. Officials came from throughout the land, from Egypt to India to Greece. The celebration was at the King's magnificent winter palace in Susa, about 200 miles North of Kuwait. It ended with a seven-day feast; King Ahasuerus hosted the men while Queen Vashti gave a banquet for the women.

On the last day of the feast, Ahasuerus, "merry with wine," called for Vashti to come to the men's party to show off her beauty, because she was a very beautiful woman. She refused and the king became furious. His counselors said that unless the king took drastic action, other women would use Vashi's refusal as an excuse to disobey their husbands, so Ahasuerus began looking for a new queen. He had the most beautiful young virgins brought to Susa where each would undergo a yearlong beauty treatment and then brought, one by one, to spend a night with the King.

Mordecai, a member of Susa's Jewish community, had adopted his young cousin Hadassah, also called Esther, when her parents died. A wise and devout man, Mordecai told Esther stories of her Jewish ancestors and of how God had brought them out of Egypt and preserved them. She was raised as a Proverbs 31 woman. Her activities were driven by the priority of caring for her people, resulted in multiplied fruitfulness for the poor and needy, her own household, herself, her husband the King and the people of her culture. Her character was strength and honor, she opened her mouth with wisdom and she looked well to the ways of her household and many people rose up and called her "Blessed." True holiness and virtue command permanent respect and affection, far more than charm and beauty of face and form.

When Esther, a beautiful young woman with a good figure, was chosen as one of the young virgins to be brought to the King, Mordecai advised her to conceal the fact that she was Jewish. After four years of looking for a new queen, Ahasuerus met Esther and "was totally smitten by her. He placed a royal crown on her head and made her queen in place of Vashti."

Some time later, King Ahasuerus appointed a new prime minister, Haman, a descendant of the enemies of the Israelites, and commanded everyone to bow down before him. Mordecai's refusal outraged Haman.

Haman learned that Mordecai was a Jew and devised a plot to kill not just Mordecai, but all the Jews in the land. A **"certain people,"** he told the King, **"do not obey the King's laws; it is not in the King's best interest to tolerate them"**

"Do with the people as you please," said Ahasuerus, and

he gave Haman his signet ring. Haman then wrote an order that in 11 months on a certain day, officials throughout the land were **"to destroy, kill, annihilate all the Jews; young and old, women and children; ...to plunder their goods."** It was the greatest attempt at Jewish genocide ever, even more drastic than Hitler's in World War 2. The Persians had an amazingly efficient postal system and the word was spread quickly throughout the land.

And Ahasuerus and Haman sat down and had a drink. But God had other plans to preserve His people.

Although Esther had been queen for more than four years when Haman issued his edict to kill all Jews, no one in the court knew she was a Jew. In a profoundly inspiring message, Mordecai told her she should not expect to escape death just because she was the wife of Ahasuerus. **"Maybe it was for a time like this that you were made queen!"**

Esther's appeal to the King would be risky. Anyone, including Esther, who approached the King without being summoned could be killed. Although she had won her husband's love and confidence, she was dealing with powerful and sinister forces. She asked Mordecai to have all the Jews in Susa spend three days in fasting and after that "I will go to the king, even though is against the law. If I must die for doing it, I will die." Esther's commitment to her people was greater than her commitment to her own life. Favor is deceitful, and beauty is vain, but a woman that feareth the LORD, she shall be praised.

After three days of prayer and fasting, Esther put on her royal robes, walked past everyone waiting for an audience with Ahasuerus, and into his presence. She could have been killed, but the King was pleased to see her. Esther invited Ahasuerus and Haman to dinner that night, where she invited them to another dinner the following night.

The next day, Esther told the King she was Jewish: **"My people and I have been sold for slaughter. If it were nothing more serious than being sold into slavery, I**

would have kept quiet; but we are about to be destroyed; exterminated!"

"Who dares to do such a thing?" demanded the King.

"This evil man Haman," she said.

One of the servants told the King that Haman had built gallows which to hang Mordecai. "Hang Haman on it!" the King commanded.

Although Haman was killed, the order to kill all Jews was still in effect. A decree sealed with the royal signet ring could not be revoked, even by the King himself. So Ahasuerus gave his signet ring to Mordecai, who issued a decree in the King's name empowering the Jews to defend themselves. **"In every city and province, wherever the King's proclamation was read, the Jews held a joyful holiday with feasting and happiness."** On the day the Jews were to be exterminated, the tables were turned and their enemies were killed.

Mordecai was made second in command in the kingdom. Ahasuerus reigned for 15 more years, and we are told no more about Esther, the courageous queen who God raised up **"for such a time as this."** Esther 1:1-10:3

The above strategies enable women to survive good business practices. Esthers understanding of palace politics easily translates into surviving in a world of corporate politics. Esther's close relationship with her cousin Mordecai, who taught her how to use her womanly talents for advancement, relates the importance of finding a trusted mentor who can serve as a guide through a man's world. And her decision to risk her own life by going against the powerful advisor Haman is a perfect example of how to deal with difficult colleagues; and when it is time to take action against them.

The greater message is that the women of the Bible, almost always, were survivors. And while they did not enjoy the same rights as men, they understood how to successfully weave their way through conflict, using feminine skills to accomplish their objectives. The above descriptions of many women can easily be applied to the myriad decisions about their life and work that women have to make every day.

Esther can also be listed under Women of Strength and Courage.

Sarah And Rebekah

Three times in Genesis a story is told of a woman's great beauty making her husband fear for his life; twice with Sarah and once with Rebekah.

Abraham and his family went to Egypt because of a famine in Canaan. Sarah, his wife, now over 65, was so beautiful that she and Abraham conspired to say that she was Abraham's sister (she actually was his half sister). He feared that if the Egyptians knew she was his wife, they would kill him. It is difficult to see her or Rebekah as a Proverbs 31 woman even though they were obedient to their husbands, but only because of life saving circumstances. In that day and time men of high authority would kill a husband just to acquire their wives if they so desired. Was physical activity initiated? Scripture does not tell us, but we can be assured that Yeshua protected Sarah and Rebekah from offensive behavior of the Egyptians.

The ruse backfired. Some Egyptian court officials saw that Sarah was amazingly beautiful and told Pharaoh about her, and Pharaoh put Sarah in his harem. Was she able to avoid Pharaoh? She stayed there long enough that Abraham became a wealthy man, accumulating sheep, cattle, donkeys, camels and servants. Pharaoh figured out that he had been deceived and kicked Abraham, Sarah and their entourage out of the country. Because taking another man's wife was taboo for Egyptians. Abraham had caused Pharaoh to sin.

About 10 years later, in another famine, they moved to Gerar, a prosperous city near today's Gaza Strip. Again, Abraham was afraid Abimelech, the King of Gerar, would kill him and take his nearly 80-year-old wife, and so they told the King they were brother and sister. The King took Sarah to be his wife, but before they slept together, God told him in a dream that Abraham and Sarah were lying. He called Abraham and asked, **"What have I ever done to you that you would bring on me and my kingdom this huge offense? What you have done to me ought never to have been done."** He then gave Sarah back to Abraham and gave him a thousand pieces of silver to clear up **"even a shadow of suspicion before the eyes of the world."**

When the story is repeated a third time, it's Isaac, Abraham's son, and his wife, Rebekah, who moved to Gerar. Because she was "so beautiful," Isaac told people that Rebekah was his sister. But when the King saw Isaac fondling Rebekah, he figured out that they were not brother and sister. **"Think of what you might have done to us! Given a little more time, one of the men might have slept with your wife; you would have been responsible for bringing guilt down on us."**
Genesis 12:10-20, 20:10-18, 26:1-11

Sarah

She was the wife of Abraham and mother of Isaac, and the principal matriarch of the Jewish people. The focus of her story is the tension between her infertility and God's promise to make her a mother of nations.

Abraham and Sarah were from Ur, a land in what is now Iraq. They had the same father, Terah, but different mothers and theirs was an arranged marriage. They did not stay in Ur because their father moved his family 650 miles to Haran in modern Turkey.

When Terah died, Abraham, age 75, Sarah, 65, and their nephew, Lot, left Haran and traveled 400 miles South to Canaan.

The first thing the Bible says about Sarah is that she "was not able to have children." She was tortured by her infertility. And yet, when God told Abraham to leave Haran, he said, **"I will give you many descendants that no one will be able to count them all."** But Abraham and Sarah had no children.

Shortly after arriving in Canaan, a famine forced Abraham and his family to go to Egypt where Sarah acquired an Egyptian Princess handmaid named Hagar. When the famine was over, Abraham returned to Canaan as an increasingly rich man.

Ten years later, when Sarah was about 75 and seemingly without hope of having a child, she suggested that Abraham sleep with Hagar. Evidently Sarah did not see any other way in which God's promises could come true, so she decided to help God out.

Hagar became pregnant right away and began to despise her mistress, the beginning of much tension between the two.

Sarah blamed Abraham **("It's your fault that Hagar despises me.")** Abraham refused to take sides: "Your maid is your business." Sarah did not appear to have a meek or quiet spirit in her treatment of Hagar and God states that the *ornament* of a meek and quiet spirit in the sight of God is a great price.

And Hagar gave birth to a son named Ishmael. Abraham delighted in Ishmael, for at last he could have descendants.

Then when Abraham was nearly 100, God told him that he would also give him a son by Sarah. **"I will bless her, and she will become the mother of nations, and there will be Kings among her descendants."**

Abraham did not believe it. **"Can a man have a child when he is 100 years old? Can Sarah have a child at ninety?**

But that is just what happened. The 90-year-old Sarah gave birth to a son named Isaac. The Renewed Testament commended Sarah for her faith because she believed God would do what he promised.

Abraham threw a big party to celebrate Isaac's having been weaned, but 14-year-old Ishmael made fun of the boy, and Sarah demanded that Abraham get rid of Hagar and Ishmael. This troubled Abraham, but God told him, **"Do whatever Sarah tells you."** She was determined to be rid of Hagar and Ishmael, and she was disobedient to her husband Abraham, not in subjection unto him. The husband is to always have the FINAL word from any intense discussion regardless of the outcome. But did Abraham show her love and make her feel secure in their relationship. A happy "tent" does not "just happen", it is the result of hard work, prayer and real affection with God at the forefront.

Sarah lived for 37 more years with Abraham and Isaac. During this time God told Abraham to offer Isaac on Mount Moriah as a burnt. Abraham prepared the altar, but at the last minute, the angel of the Lord stopped him and said to sacrifice instead a ram that was caught in a nearby thicket. *"Because you have not refused to give me your son, your dear, dear son,"* the angel said, *"all nations on Earth will find themselves blessed through your descendants because you obeyed me."*

Sarah died in Hebron and Abraham bought a cave there to bury her. When Abraham died, Isaac and Ishmael, in a momentary reconciliation, together buried Abraham in the same cave.

The Apostle Peter in describing Sarah, the mother of the Jewish people, held her up as an example for wives: **"Let your adornment...be the hidden person of the heart, with the incorruptible beauty of a gentle and quiet spirit, which is very precious in the sight of God."**
Genesis 11:27-13:2, 16:1-16, 17:15-22, 20:1-21, 23:1-2, 19-20.

Daughters Of Job

Job, the richest man in the East, had seven sons and three daughters. He was an honest man and devoted to God. But satan believed Job's devotion was due to God having blessed him with so much. With God's permission, satan took away everything Job had. His servants, his cattle, his camels, his donkeys and even his sons and daughters were all killed. And then satan took away Job's health. Please note, Galatians 6:7-8. 7 Be not deceived; God is not mocked, for whatsoever a man soweth, that shall he also reap. 8. For he that soweth to his flesh shall of the flesh reap corruption, but he that soweth to the Spirit shall of the Spirit reap life everlasting.

Satan was proven wrong. After Job had lost everything that mattered to him, his wife said to him, **"You are still as faithful as ever, aren't you? Why don't you curse God and die?"** But Job remained faithful to God: **"I know that my Redeemer lives, and at the last he will stand upon the Earth. And after my skin has been thus destroyed, yet in my flesh I shall see God."**

Having proved his faith, Job received from God twice the number of sheep, camels and donkeys he had had before. Job had seven more sons and three more daughters. The daughters were very special for, in an unusual move at the time, Job gave each of them a share of the inheritance along with their brothers. **"There were no other women in the whole world as beautiful as Job's daughters."** Even their names suggest beauty: Jemimah means **"dove,"** Keziah refers to a variety of cinnamon used as a **perfume**, and Keren Happuch means a small box used for **eye makeup.** Job 1:1-2:10; 42:10-17

Women Who Didn't Start Off As A Proverbs 31 Woman But Grew Into One

All of the following women are listed above in other Sections of this Book.

Sarah – Beautiful Women of the Bible
Abigail – Beautiful Women of the Bible
Rahab – Beautiful Women of the Bible
Esther – Beautiful Women of the Bible

Rebekah – Beautiful Women of the Bible
Rachel – Beautiful Women of the Bible

Bathsheba

We know very little about her even though she is one of the most famous women of the Bible. She was listed as "very beautiful". She was the wife of Uriah the Hittite, a soldier in David's army and a man of honor, integrity and character. She apparently did not start out being a Proverbs 31 woman but many years later, did show herself to be a remarkable woman.

Without exception, King David evidently liked beautiful women. He was already married to Abigail, one of the most beautiful women in the world. David had six other wives: **Michal,** daughter of King Saul, was David's first wife, she had no children. **Ahinoam of Jezreel** the mother of Amnon. **Maachah** daughter of the King of Geshur and mother of Absalom. **Haggith** mother of Adonijah, who later claimed the throne of his father. **Abital** mother of Shephatiah. **Eglah** mother of Ithream. And **Abigail** was the widow of Nabal and mother of Chileab, which made 7 wives. Were these women Proverbs 31 women? We really have no way of knowing except for Abigail and Bathsheba.

Bathsheba made number 8 and was the mother of Solomon. These first seven women all married David before he moved his capital to Jerusalem. After building his palace, he married **Bathsheba,** mother of King Solomon; the wisest man in the world. Bathsheba may have suffered from a man that was at first carnal and worldly, like Uriah and then David. Scripture does not tell us. The Bible knows nothing of a "double standard" for husbands and wives. Bathsheba learned that David was spiritual, loyal, industrious and a man after God's very own heart. In God's gracious plan, He has ordered that both husband and wife are needed in the home and that each one must fulfill certain ministries. One cannot replace the other, although in some emergencies (such as death of one mate) God has given grace for a person to be both "father and mother" in the home. However, such arrangements are, at their best, less than ideal. God obviously honored Bathsheba and David's union as He gave them Solomon, whom was the wisest King in all earth.

Roofs had a special significance in Scriptures. There were roofs for ripening fruits and vegetables, drying flax, and no doubt drying the wash too. They could be used for praying or for sleeping when the heat made indoor quarters uncomfortable. A roof could also be a social center, a place to gossip with one's neighbor, and a spot from which to survey the passing scene. From such a vantage point, David saw Bathsheba bathing and his lust for her was aroused. David had arose from a nap and he looked down and saw a "stunningly beautiful" woman bathing in her own courtyard where she had expected privacy. Bathsheba was making sure she was clean after menstruating, as required by Jewish ritual regulations. There is nothing in the Bible to suggest that Bathsheba was luring David into the relationship. Instead, she apparently became a victim of his lust.

The story is told with remarkably little detail: **"He saw...he asked about her...he sent to get her...she arrived, he went to bed with her...she returned home."** That's it! No love, no foreplay. King David took what he wanted. But Bathsheba **"later sent word to David: I'm pregnant."**

David then compounded his disobedience. Twice he tried to arrange for Uriah to have sex with Bathsheba so it could be said that the baby's father was Uriah. When that failed, David arranged to have Uriah killed in battle.

When Bathsheba learned that Uriah was dead, she grieved, and then David took this beautiful woman to be his wife, and she bore his son. Because of David's disobedience, the child died, much to the grief of both David and Bathsheba. Their second son was Solomon, followed by three more. If the story had ended here, it would have been a tale of might makes right, and the pursuit of pleasure being the privilege of the upper class.

But Bathsheba's role in Solomon becoming King shows a lesser-known but more interesting side of her. When David was old and dying, his fourth son, Adonijah, declared that he was King. He rounded up his supporters and even had a coronation feast without telling his father. Adonijah was usurping David's wishes because David had said he wanted Solomon to succeed him.

The prophet Nathan told Queen Bathsheba, who had influence in the royal court, to tell David about Adonijah's seizing the throne. She went to David's bedroom, told him that **"every eye in Israel is watching to see what you'll do,"** and said **"if you fail to act, the moment you're buried my son Solomon and I am as good as dead."** **As a Proverbs 31 woman she obviously had David's back and also her son. Bathsheba and David had a deep soul relationship, they loved each other deeply.**

Nathan then verified Bathsheba's story.

David called Bathsheba back and said, **"Your son Solomon will be King after me and take my place on the throne. And I'll make sure it happens this very day."**

Bathsheba demonstrated wisdom, finesse, courtesy and vision in this encounter; qualities that we did not see when she and David first met. She became a Proverbs 31 woman, she was David's friend, soul mate and had his back. She was him in another body. She then became the Queen Mother and was given all the honors and dignities she deserved. Of David's eight wives, she was the most honored.
11 Samuel 11:1-12:24, 1 Kings 1:5-40, 2:13-24

Rachel

The story of Rachel and Jacob is one of the most beautiful love stories in the Bible. Rachel was taking care of her sheep when she met her cousin Jacob, who had just arrived in Haran from his home more than 400 miles to the South. She was described as **"shapely and beautiful,"** and they instantly fell in love. Jacob kissed her, wept for joy and agreed to work for her father, Laban, for seven years for her hand in marriage, although **"It seemed like only a few days because he loved her so much."**

But just as Jacob had tricked his Father, Isaac, into giving Isaac's blessing to him instead of to Esau (see Rebekah's story in Genesis Chapter 27) Laban tricked Jacob. The bride wore a veil on her wedding night and it was not until the next morning that Jacob realized he had married Rachel's older sister, Leah. He then married Rachel too, but committed to seven more years of work for Laban.

After many years, Jacob had 10 sons, but none by Rachel, whom he still loved passionately. Her agony was unbearable. **"Give me children, or I will die."** God answered Rachel's desire; she gave birth to Joseph and then she died giving birth to Benjamin. She was buried just outside of Bethlehem, where her tomb remains today. It is hard to believe that she or Leah (her sister) were Proverbs 31 women because of their behavior not only toward each other but their husband, Jacob.
Genesis 29:1-30:24, 35:16-20

Wedding Traditions From The Bible

Jewish weddings take place under a canopy without sides, called a chuppah, because supposedly Sarah and Abraham had their tent opened to welcome all with hospitality. Other scholars believe this custom has been handed down from the book of Ruth, in which Ruth tells Boaz, her future husband, to "spread your robe over" her.

While purely arranged marriages the type of "shidduch" that brought Isaac and Rebekah together, are rare, Orthodox Jewish families still often use matchmakers to introduce suitable marriage candidates.

The tradition of a simple, unadorned wedding band may refer to the apostle Peter's message to Christian women that true beauty cannot be found in "that outward adorning of plaiting of the hair, and of wearing of gold or of putting on (fashionable clothing) but let it be the hidden man of the heart..."

The use of a veil also appears to derive from the Bible. In Orthodox ceremonies, the groom places a veil, called a "badeken," over his bride's face. This supposedly refers to the story in Genesis in which Rebecca covered her face when she first saw Isaac, her intended husband. Some scholars believe it also is done to ensure that the groom is marrying the correct woman, referring to the story of Jacob, who was tricked into marrying Laban's oldest daughter, Leah, rather his intended bride, Rachel. Who can find a virtuous woman? For her price is far above rubies. Proverbs 31:10 Listed are some concepts of a virtuous woman, you decide. She does exist, she simply must be found as Jacob found Rachel at the well. She was one among thousands, not average. She was not common or normal. She was not a black eyes wild flower or dandelion to be blown haphazardly into the wind. What the average woman will do, she REFUSES to do. She waited 7 years for Jacob. She does not even respond to the same kind of man the average woman responds to and what makes an average woman angry, makes her THOUGHTFUL. Rachel's thoughts were different, her motives were different and her conduct and behavior were different, even toward the other 3 women in Jacob's life. We need to remember that in that day and time, women were PROPERTY and each one had value.

Women Of Strength And Courage

Deborah

The Judges were Othniel, Eduh, Shamgar. The fourth judge of Israel was Deborah, who was also a prophetess. Then Gideon, the minor Judges (Tola and Jair), Jephthah, 3 minor Judges, (Ibzan, Elon, Abdon and Samson.

Little is known about Deborah except that she sat under

a palm tree arbitrating disputes among the people, speaking words of encouragement and wisdom. It requires a Proverbs 31 woman to be a woman of strength and courage. Her husband had to be a rare man capable of discerning who she was. Because of the uniqueness of her, how she thinks, how she considers the ways of the LORD through Torah, how she worked and spoke wisdom. It takes a man who fears the LORD to begin to see or even understand who and what she really is. And why she is the jewel of great price.

The Israelites had been oppressed for 20 years by King Jabin of Hazor and his powerful general, Sisera. According to Jewish legend, Sisera never lost a battle. When he shouted, solid walls would shake and wild animals would be petrified. When he bathed in a river, his beard would catch enough fish to feed his whole army. King Jabin's army would be like using spears against a modern army.

God told Deborah to free her people from the oppression of Jabin, so she told Barak, her military general, to get 10,000 men to fight Sisera. **"I'll make sure you win the battle,"** she said.

But Barak was a bit of a wimp. **"If you go with me, I'll go. But if you don't do with me, I won't go."**

Deborah had fire in her eyes and strength in her voice when she said, **"Of course I'll go with you. But understand that with an attitude like that, there'll be no glory in it for you. God will use a woman's hand to take care of Sisera."** Her words were more than just inspiring leadership. They were also prophetic.

Barak marched his 10,000 men to the top of Mount Tabor. When Sisera started after Barak, it began to rain. Deborah gave the signal, and all 10,000 men swept down the mountain. Sisera's men panicked and drove their 900 chariots of iron toward the Kishon river, where they became bogged down in the mud due to heavy rain mixed with sleet and hail. Sisera's army was defeated and all of his soldiers were killed.

Fleeing for his life, Sisera stopped at the tent of Jael,

who he mistakenly thought was an ally of Jabin. Jael, however, was aware of Jabin's cruel treatment of the Jews. She gave the exhausted Sisera some milk, covered him with a blanket and made sure he was comfortable. **"Stand at the door of the tent,"** he said. **"If anyone comes and asks you if anyone is here, say no."**

When Sisera was sound asleep, Jael killed him by hammering a tent peg through his skull. When Barak arrived, looking for Sisera, Jael greeted him: **"Come here! I'll show you the man you're looking for,"** fulfilling Deborah's prophecy. It was the first great victory for the Israelites since the death of Joshua more than 100 years earlier. The greatest tribute to Deborah was that there was peace in the land for forty years.

The oldest example of Hebrew poetry, the "Song of Deborah" in the fifth chapter of Judges, is a victory hymn sung by Deborah and Barak.

Deborah's gifts of prophecy and leadership skill made her a woman of great strength and courage. At a critical time in Israel's history, she and Jael saved their people with a victory over their oppressors. Deborah took charge, inspired her troops in battle, judged fairly and wisely and was steadfast and loyal to God. Judges 4:1-5; 5:31

The Bleeding Woman

A large crowd was waiting for Jesus and his disciples when they returned to Galilee from the land of Garasene. They were also met by Jairus, a ruler of a synagogue in Capernaum who threw himself at Jesus' feet and begged him to heal his daughter who was deathly ill:
"My dear daughter is a death's door. Come and lay hands on her so she will get well and live." Mark 5:21-24

Jesus went with him and his disciples helping him push through the jostling crowd that thronged the narrow streets of Capernaum, when he felt a touch. Not just any touch, but a touch of the faithful; a furtive touch that took the power of healing from Jesus. He stopped ad looked around asking, **"Who touched me?"**

His disciples were puzzled as there were dozens of people surrounding them and when no one answered, Peter said, **"But Master, we've got crowds of people on our hands. Dozens have touched you."** Luke 8:43-45

Jesus, however, insisted that someone had touched him and demanded the person step forward. He had felt the power leave him and he knew that a faithful person had been healed. Finally, a woman prostrated herself before him, trembling in fear, and told her story. She had been bleeding for 12 long years and none had been able to heal her though she had sought out the best doctors and paid them well for their labors. She was bleeding from a woman's place and hence was thought unclean, therefore her fear. But she believed. Her faith was strong. She had come to Capernaum because she believed that all she had to do was touch the merest part of him. The hem of his garment, the fringe of his cloak (his prayer shawl), and she would be healed. Indeed, it had happened. The faintest touch of her hand on him, and she could feel the change. The flow of blood dried up and she had felt herself healed.

Jesus reassured her. **"Courage daughter. You took a risk of faith, and now you're well."** Matthew 9:22 She was considered unclean, but Jesus was her only hope. She desired a relationship with her family, so change mattered to her. The same words, the same friends, the sameness will paralyze one and she wanted to be well. Healed completely of bleeding and Jesus provided that because she had courage for mastering her day. She was focused and had a plan, which was accomplished. She was a Proverbs 31 woman in many ways. She made a decision that created the future she deeply wanted. Do we have that kind of courage?

She probably hid because she wanted to remain anonymous. In the society of her time, a menstruating woman was considered unclean. She should not have been out in public. Did she go to Capernaum alone and disguised? Likely so.

Medically speaking, she may have had endometrial polyps in her uterus that caused the bleeding or the more serious obstetric fistula (where a hole develops between the wall of the bladder and the vagina, usually during childbirth, and does not heal). Regardless, she should not have been out, much less trying to touch a revered celebrity of the time. That she also considers herself unclean is obvious as she does not dare actually approach Jesus for help but hides in the crowd and sneaks up from behind, reaching out to touch the fringe of his robe, to steal healing from him. She is also afraid to reveal herself at first when Jesus calls for the one who touched him to show him or herself, but finally kneels to confess, trembling with fear.

Why was his nameless woman healed? In the throng of humanity that waited to see Jesus that crowded around him, and the dozens of people that actually touched him, surely that had to be one with a scratch, a cut or a minor ailment. But Jesus only felt his power discharge when this particular woman touched him, and it boils down to faith. For 12 years this woman had suffered, and it boils down to faith. For 12 years this woman had suffered, and paid through her nose for he best physicians who only left her poorer for the effort. She had faith in Jesus' power to heal, so much that she believed all she had to do was touch him. She said to herself, **"If I can put a finger on his robe, (prayer shawl) I can get well."**

We see that Jesus could feel his power discharge. He also knew that only someone with true faith could have done it. Dozens must have pressed against him in the crowd, yet he kept asking who it was that had touched him. Then, when he finds out who it was and why he had been touched, he did not berate the woman for wanting his power, he did not revile her for her unclean condition. Jesus shows an inordinate amount of grace for a man at his time for he understands the taboos of the day as well as any other. He instead calls her

"daughter," praises her faith and wishes her well. Would our faith be as strong?

Ruth

She is a sweet story with no murder, war or violence. It is a beautiful story of friendship and romance, of Ruth's commitment to her mother-in-law Naomi and of Boaz's love for Ruth. She did not give an ultimatum to Boaz about marriage, he made the decision. She followed the advise of an older woman, her Mother-in-law Naomi and she became the mother of Obed and the grandmother of David.

When a famine came to Bethlehem, Elimelech, Naomi and their two sons moved to Moah, on the East side of the Dead Sea. Elimelech died and despite Jewish prohibitions about marrying non-Jewish women, the two sons married Orpah and Ruth, who, tradition says, were the daughters of the King of Moab.

During their 10 years of marriage, Ruth loved her husband and her mother-in-law and learned about their God. When both sons died, Naomi and her two daughters-in-law struggled to survive. The famine in Bethlehem had ended, and Naomi decided to return. She was too old to remarry, but she encouraged Orpah and Ruth to stay in Moab, find good husbands and bear children. Orpad did, but Ruth replied with one of the most beautiful speeches ever written:

"Intreat me not leave thee, or to return from following after thee: for whither thou goest, I will go; and where thou lodgest, I will lodge: thy people thy people shall be my people, and thy God my God: Where thou diest, will I die, and there will I be buried: the Lord do so to me, and more also, if ought but death part thee and me."

Ruth showed no self-pity, but a sweetness of spirit, affection for her husband and a loyalty to his mother, his people, his country and his God. After a difficult journey around the Dead Sea and through the Judean wilderness,

Naomi and Ruth were welcomed in Bethlehem. **"Don't call me Naomi"** (which means "sweet), Naomi said to her friends. **"Call me bitter"** because **"the Almighty has brought calamity upon me."**

Ruth and Naomi were penniless, so Ruth became a gleaner, picking up barley and wheat left by reapers. Proverbs 31:17 says, She gathers her strength around her and throws herself into her work. She was not afraid of work. One of the fields she worked belonged to Boaz, a rich and influential relative of Naomi's husband. Boaz told Ruth to glean in his fields. He said he would make sure his young men did not bother her and she could drink his water. He had heard how kind she had been to Naomi. Ruth said, **"How does this happen that you should pick me out and treat me so kindly; me, a foreigner? You've touched my heart, treated me like one of your own. And I don't even belong here!"**

When Ruth reported to Naomi what had happened, Naomi said, **"Why, God bless that man! God hasn't quite walked out on us after all! He still loves us, in bad times as well as good! That man, Ruth, is a close relative of ours!"**

Naomi realized that according to the custom of levirate marriage, Ruth could expect her husband's closest male relative to marry her. So she told Ruth to **"wash yourself, put on some perfume and get dressed in your best clothes. Then go to where he is threshing, but don't let him know you are there until he has finished eating and drinking."**

Ruth did not let Boaz see her, but when he sent to sleep by a stack of barley, she quietly lay down, and when he wakes up in the middle of the night, asked him to **"take me under your protecting wing."**

"God bless you. What a splendid expression of love! And when you could have had your pick of any of he young men around. Everybody in town knows what a courageous woman you are."

Boaz and Ruth married and had a son, Obed, who was the grandfather of King David.

Like a chorus in a Greek play, the own women brought closure to the story, for Naomi's life was no longer bitter, but sweet: **"Praise the Lord! He has given you a grandson today to take care of you. May the boy become famous in Israel! Your daughter-in-law loves you, and has done more for you than seven sons. And now she has given you a grandson, who will bring new life to you and give you security in your old age."**
Ruth 1:1-4:22

Gleaning

Gleaning is the act of collecting leftover crops from farmers' fields. In biblical times, reapers would cut grain with wooden sickles that had blades of sharpened flint. Binders then tied the stalks of grain in bundles called sheaves. The heads of the grain for food would be separated from the stalks used for straw.

Ruth was a Proverbs 31 woman. Proverbs 31:18 says, She perceiveth that her merchandise is good, her candle goeth not out by night. Her product was excellent. She did not wait for others to reassure her. She did not require that Boaz be an incessant cheerleader in her life. He did not need to hold her hand and speak effusive compliments into her ears, even though he praises her, which he did. She was at peace and walked in excellence.

Gleaners would pick up any straw or grain missed by the other workers. Gleaning was back breaking work in the hot sun. In a sense, gleaning was a form of welfare system because Old Testament law required property owners to leave the gleanings "for poor people and foreigners."

Gleaning was not just practiced in biblical times. In 19th century England, for instance, churches frequently rang a "gleaning bell" at 8 a.m. and 7 p.m., so that the gleaners would have an opportunity to pick up leftovers. Food banks are a modern form of gleaning in which donated food is distributed to the needy.

Jochebed, Mother Of Moses

If the effectiveness of a mother is demonstrated in the lives of her children, Jochebed is the greatest mother in the Old Testament. All three of her children (Miriam, Aaron, and Moses) helped guide the Children of Israel when they left Egypt for the Promised Land. However, we do not know much about Jochebed herself.

When Jacob moved to Egypt at the invitation of Pharaoh, there were only 70 people in his family. But their descendants, the Israelites, had so many children that "the land was filled with them." Years later, a new Pharaoh feared that the Hebrews might become more numerous than the Egyptians and told midwives to kill every male Jewish baby. The midwives did not obey the order, so Pharaoh told Egyptians to throw Jewish baby boys in the Nile River.

Jochebed, wife of Amram, a Levite, was determined not to let her third child, Moses die. For three months she kept him quiet. When he became too active to keep hidden, she waterproofed a small boat made of papyrus, placed the baby in it and put it afloat among some reeds at the edge of the Nile. His older sister, Miriam, hid in the nearby reeds. A Proverbs 31 woman had the KNOWLEDGE of the necessary equipment to do what she needed to do. She had the determination to put the little basket ark together. She was OBSERVANT. She reached out and protected her baby son who grew up to be a great prophet and deliver, Moses. She thought ahead and also taught his older sister the necessity of protecting him at the river. They loved God and trusted him in all His wisdom. She went above and beyond being a Proverbs 31 woman.

When Pharaoh's daughter came to the Nile to bathe, she saw the small boat and found the baby Moses. Her heart went out to him, even though she knew he was a Hebrew boy who should be drowned. Miriam asked Pharaoh's daughter if she wanted a wet nurse for the baby; and then ran to get Jochebed.

Jochebed was able to take care of her own son and was paid to do it! Until he was about 3 years old, Moses lived with his parents, his sister and his older brother, Aaron, in the family's flimsy reed hut. His parents were Hebrew slaves and when not farming, his father probably made bricks for Egyptian buildings. However, during those first 3 formative years, Jochebed instilled in Moses a love of God. She recounted stories of Abraham's faith in moving to the Promised Land, of the miraculous birth of Moses' ancestor Isaac, of Abraham's obeying God's command to sacrifice his son and the miraculous provision of a ram, of Joseph's rise to power after being sold to traders. Jochebed taught God's commands to Moses **"when at home and when away, when resting and when working."** It is certain that Amram also had an important part in Moses upbringing as a Jewish Father would.

When Moses no longer needed a nurse, Pharaoh's daughter raised him as an Egyptian prince. He lived in a palace and, at about 6 years old, was sent to the temple school to learn to write using hieroglyphics and to memorize classical Egyptian writings. He ate the best food and wore the finest clothes.

Jochebed and Amram had three children as stated. Miriam, the oldest, was a brilliant and courageous prophetess who helped guide the Israelites in the wilderness. She is known for leading "all the women" in a song of deliverance after crossing the Red Sea. Later she criticized Moses when he married an Ethiopian woman, and as a result, God struck her with leprosy. But Moses spoke to God on her behalf and she was healed.

Aaron was the spokesperson when he and Moses went before Pharaoh demanding that the Israelites should be let go. Although Aaron was the first high priest of Israel, he made a golden calf for the people to worship while Moses was on Mount Sinai receiving the Ten Commandments. God was furious with Aaron, but once again, Moses spoke to God and Aaron was spared God's wrath.

Moses was one of the most important men in the Old Testament. God chose him to lead the Israelites out of Egypt. He received the Ten Commandment and the rest of God's law. And as author of the first five books of the Bible, he wrote more of the Bible than any other person.

Surely Jochebed, the mother of Miriam, Aaron and Moses, can lay claim to being the greatest mother in the Bible, except for Mary, the mother of Jesus and Elizabeth, the mother of John the Baptist.
Exodus 2:1-10

Remarkable Women (Mothers)

Preparation of the heart is an ongoing process. It involves holding the heart out before the Lord with an attitude of desiring to please Him in all areas of our lives. It also involves accepting the inevitability of change in our lives, saying to God: "Prepare my heart, Lord, for what you have in store for me. I trust that any change initiated by you is for the better, no matter how it appears at the time. Help me to yield to your plans for my life and others, which are always good and full of hope." The following Remarkable Mothers did just exactly that. Proverbs 16:1 address that, "The preparations of the heart belong to man, but the answer of the tongue is from the LORD."

Hannah

She was a godly woman and mother whose life was marked by faith and perseverance, a Proverbs 31 woman in every way. But it was not easy. Her agony about being childless was made worse by a taunting rival and a husband who meant well but did not understand her. The depth of

Hannah's sorrow made the eventual birth of her son even more wonderful.

Hannah was one of two wives of Elkanah, a good man who was an assistant to the priests. He loved Hannah, but she did not have any children, so Elkanah married Peninnah, who gave birth to many sons and daughters.

Every year the entire family went to Shiloh, where the Ark of the Covenant was kept in the Tabernacle, for a week long feast. During these times Peninnah made fun of Hannah, not letting her forget that she was barren. Peninnah's taunting upset Hannah' she was reduced to tears and not able to eat.

Hannah was the love of Elkanah's life, but he did not understand her agony: **"Hannah, why are you crying? Why won't you eat? Why are you always so sad? Don't I mean more to you than ten sons?"** He meant well, but he did not quite understand that a mother's relationship with her children is quite different from a wife's relationship with her husband.

After dinner, Hannah slipped away to the Tabernacle, where she cried inconsolably and prayed. Her rival mocked her, her husband did not understand her. She pleaded with God to look at her pain and promised if God "gives me a son, I'll give him completely, unreservedly to you. I'll set him apart for a life of holy discipline." Hannah was completely open with God in her heartbreak and serious with God in her promise.

Eli, the high priest, saw Hannah praying and thought she was drunk. **"Stop your drinking and sober up!"** he said. Hannah explained that she had not been drinking, but pouring out her heart directly to God. **"I have been praying like this because I'm so miserable."**

"Go in peace," Eli said, realizing his mistake, **"and may the God of Israel give you what you have asked him for."**

Elkanah and his family got up early the next morning, worshipped God and returned home. Elkanah and Hannah slept together, and God allowed her to become pregnant. Within the year Samuel was born.

After Samuel was weaned, Hannah took him to Shiloh, worshipped God and left him with Eli, who taught Samuel to perform certain duties dressed in a priestly linen tunic. Every year Hannah would lovingly make a new tunic for the growing boy and take it to Shiloh. Eli blessed Hannah and her husband, asking God to give them more children **"to take the place of the one you dedicated to him."** Hannah and Elkanah had three more sons and two daughters.

We do not hear anymore about Hannah, but Samuel went on to become one of the most important leaders of Israel and the judge who anointed Saul, the first King of Israel.

It is hard to miss the parallels in the stories of Hannah and Mary, the mother of Jesus. Both women conceived through a miracle of God. Both women praised God with a magnificent song: Hannah's is in 1 Samuel 2:1-10 and Mary's is in Luke 1:46-55. Both dedicated their sons to the Lord: 1 Samuel 1:24-28 and Luke 2:22-24.

We are told that their sons "gained favor both with the Lord and with people" (Samuel) and grew **"in both body and spirit, blessed by both God and people" (Jesus).** And both sons were anointed by God: Samuel to become one of the greatest leaders of Israel, and Jesus to offer himself for our salvation" so that everyone who believes in him may not die but have eternal life."
1 Samuel 1:1-2:11

Lois And Eunice: They were Proverbs 31 women.

Although there are many grandmothers in the Bible, the term "grandmother" is used for only one: Lois. She was the mother of Eunice, who was the mother of Timothy, a protégé of the Apostle Paul on his missionary journeys. Lois and Eunice are mentioned in only one verse, but the powerful influence they had on young Timothy is clear.

Timothy was born in Lystra, a frontier outpost in central Turkey inhabited by Greeks, Jews, Roman soldiers and native Lycaonians. Although Lystra did not have enough Jews for a synagogue, Eunice was raised in a devout Jewish home. Either out of rebellion or a lack of options, she married a Greek man who did not share her faith. Timothy, their son, was not circumcised, as he surely would have been had his father converted to Judaism.

Eunice wanted to teach young Timothy the Bible, but, like most parents, she needed help in relaying its facts and demonstrating its principles. Eunice enlisted her own mother, Lois. Both mother and grandmother knew the Old Testament stories and the essential teachings of the Jewish faith. A godly grandmother prays for a child reinforces the parents' teaching, supports their decisions and becomes an important part of the child's life. And Lois was a godly grandmother.

Eunice also enlisted the help of believers in her community. They got to know Timothy and mentored him so that Luke could report that Timothy **"was well spoken of by the brethren who were at Lystra."**

When the Apostle Paul came to Lystra and healed a man, the people thought that the gods were visiting them. They said Paul was Hermes, and Barnabas, Paul's associate, was Zeus and they began to prepare a sacrifice to them. The adulation did not last because the crowd turned on them. They stoned Paul and dragged him outside the town, where they left him for dead.

Lois, Eunice and Timothy heard Paul preach, perhaps during this brief time in Lystra or in a synagogue in a nearby town, and they became followers of Jesus.

On his second visit to Lysra, Paul asked Timothy to accompany him on his preaching mission. First, though, he had Timothy circumcised to make him acceptable to the Jews living nearby because they knew that Timothy's father was Greek. Later Paul lovingly called Timothy **"my son in the faith."**

Lois and Eunice are mentioned only once in the Bible, but their influence on the young Timothy profoundly affected the ministry of the Apostle Paul. Lois and Eunice are an inspiration to mothers and grandmothers to give a good example, sound teaching and lots of love to their children.

Paul may have had the example of Lois and Eunice in mind when he wrote to Timothy to **"Teach believers with your life: by word, by demeanor, by love, by faith, by integrity. Stay at your post reading Scripture, giving counsel, teaching. And that special gift of ministry you were given when the leaders of the church laid hands on you and prayed; keep that dusted off and in use."**
11 Timothy 1:5

Sarah
It is also worthy to note that Sarah is another one of those Remarkable Women (Mothers) in the Bible!
Genesis 11:27;13:2;16:1-16;17:15-22;18:1-15;20:1-21;23:1-2;19-20.

Widow At Nain
The term "Nain" or "Naim" in Hebrew means "pleasant, lovely, sweet, delightful," and throughout Scriptures it refers to lights or pleasure, pleasant places, sweet words and the loveliness of making love. It is also used to refer to the pleasant harmonious concord of friends or family: **"Behold, how good and how pleasant it is for brethren to dwell together in unity!"** Psalm 133:1.

Jesus views interruptions as opportunities. He arived a Nain, and with his disciples, was blocked off in the street by a noisy funeral procession. Instead of becoming angry or bothered, Jesus watched with compassion. He chose to care, and he chose to involve himself and express his care in a tangible way.

Jesus honors mothers. Throughout Jesus' ministry, he revered mothers. He heard the Canaanite woman's plea to cast out the demon from her daughter, he healed Peter's mother of her fever and he told the disciples to let the mothers bring their little children and babies to him. Even on the tree (cross), Jesus looked out for his own mother, telling John to take care of Mary. This story is no different.

Jesus values women, all women and especially Proverbs 31 women. In a historical and cultural framework that did not acknowledge full inheritance rights to women, to lose a husband would mean loss of home and land and money and family for the woman, unless there was an heir. With a son, the inheritance passed on, and her life and sustenance could continue with him. But if there was no son, or if the son died, she forfeited everything. To be a widow brought sorrow, but to be a widow without a son brought calamity.

Jesus loves widows. The Lord, unlike pagan gods, promised to administer justice for the fatherless and the widow. And a messianic prophecy says, **"You will forget the shame of your youth, and will not remember the reproach of your widowhood anymore. For your Makes is your husband, the Lord of hosts is His name, and your Redeemer is the Holy One of Israel; He is called the God of the whole earth. For the Lord has called you like a woman forsaken and grieved in spirit."** Isaiah 54:4-6

Jesus saw this bereaved mother's tears and heard her cries. He knew what her plight would be. And his heart moved to action.

The view in this village was anything but "lovely." It was marred by a funeral procession, and the typical sweet music was replaced by laments and wailing. A widow's only son was being carried out for burial. *When Jesus saw her, his heart broke. He said to her,* **"Don't cry."** *Then he went over and touched the coffin. The pallbearers stopped. He said,* **"Young man, I tell you. Get up."** *The dead son sat up and began talking. Jesus presented him to his mother. Luke 7:13-15*

Nain once again became lovely with added reverence

and awe. *They all realized they were in a place of holy mystery, that God was at work among them. They were quietly worshipful; and then noisily grateful calling out among themselves,* **"God is back, looking to the needs of his people!"** *The news of Jesus spread all through the country.* Luke 7:16-17

The city of Nain; and the widow there; appears only once in the Bible. But these short verses, together with the cultural and biblical context of Jesus' life, paint a breathtaking lovely picture of Jesus' compassion and care for the hurting. Indeed, the story is "nain me'od" or very lovely.

If you travel to Nain today, the only evidence you find of the widow is an old highway sign and the Franscian church which contains two lovely paintings depicting Jesus resurrecting her son.

Canaanite Woman

Who was this woman? A native of Greece, as a Syrophoenician, she was considered "upper class" in her own community. But what did that matter to these religious leaders? They thought of people like her as no better than dogs. No woman, especially unaccompanied, would dare approach a man, let alone a rabbi, lest she thought a prostitute. But who would go with her to talk to the master? No one.

But why would a man with such miraculous gifts, this man people said had literally come down from heaven, heal only Jewish children? Surely she could appeal to his conscience. It had to be worth a try.

There was one more thing people were saying about him. Many thought he was the one, the long-awaited Messiah who would save his people. She read the Holy Scriptures and all the signs pointed to him being this prophesied son of David. She obviously had read and knew Torah. Proverbs 31:25 describes her beautifully. 25 "Strength and honor are her clothing, and she shall rejoice in time to come." She was not afraid to approach him even in the light of rejection for He was a Messiah of healing and restoration and she knew that. She trusted him completely. Her trust was rewarded.

And then she heard he was in the area, staying at a home not far away. Oh, there were people everywhere trying to get close to him. How could she make his happen?

"Have mercy, son of David!" she cried out. Yet he ignored her, dismissed her, even called her a dog. His followers called her a nuisance and asked the Master to send her away. She heard him say to his disciples. **"I've got my hands full dealing with the lost sheep of Israel."** Maybe he was no different from the others after all. She knew in her heart that He was different.

With her persistent faith what more did she have to lose? After all, she was a person with feeling and needs and a daughter whom she loved who needed what only this man could give. She was not too proud to beg him for it. Throwing herself on her knees before him, she poured out her heart once more. **"Have mercy, son of David."**

Acknowledging her, he said. "It's not right to take bread out of children's mouths and throw it to dogs. She was quick: You're right, Master, but beggar dogs do get scraps from the master's table." Matthew 15:26-27

That was all he'd been waiting to hear. Jesus of Nazareth looked at her with a heart full of compassion and spoke words no one expected to hear.

"Oh, woman," he said, **"Your faith is something else. What you want is what you get!"**" Right then her daughter became well. Matthew 15:28 Her reward was that she was obedient to Torah and faithfully followed it. Was she an Israelite? Maybe so, maybe not. But she looked well to the ways of her household and her children will rise up and call her blessed.

Do the attitudes of the religious leaders that day toward this woman sound like positions we still encounter today? Have you ever been looked down on or called names by anyone? Do you ever feel like the Canaanite woman, as if you are not "good enough" to fit in with a certain group of that somehow you are not worthy of God's love? People often do not change until they are confronted with the wrongness of their thinking. That is the lesson we learn from the Canaanite woman, that no one has to put up with bullying attitudes or with those who attempt to exclude them.

No person is greater or less than any other. We are all the same in God's eyes. It does not matter where we come from, what our cultural or family history is, what we look like or any other thing about us. All that matters is that we recognize ourselves and others as equally deserving of compassion. Because this woman believed that truth, her daughter was set free from her troubles, and her story has been told the world over ever since.

Women Who Sang the Blues

There are plenty of stories that do not make us feel very good because the people in them have been abused, rejected and done wrong. These are the Bible stories for adults, for the people who have been abused, rejected and done wrong.

Hagar

She was the mother of Abraham's first son, Ishmael. Sarah was the mother of his second son, Isaac. Tension between the two women erupted and Hagar and her teenage son were driven into the wilderness, where it was probably expected that they would die.

God said about Ishmael, **"I'm going to make of him a great nation."** God also told Abraham about Sarah **"Nations will come from her."** From Ishmael came the Arabs; from Isaac came the Jews. Today's conflict began between the mothers of Ishmael and Isaac, even before their births.

Tradition says that Hagar, the daughter of Pharaoh, was given to Sarah because of the embarrassment caused when

Pharaoh mistakenly took Sarah for his wife. Abraham and Sarah went back to Hebron, taking with them the riches Abraham had accumulated in Egypt, and Hagar, who had no choice in the matter.

Hagar, who had been brought up as royalty in a sophisticated Egyptian city, became a handmaid in an isolated nomadic community, forced to do whatever her mistress commanded. She could not make a choice in the matter. She was given away like a piece of meat to Sarah in order to appease Abraham. As stated before, women were considered goods, a piece of baggage, a piece of property to keep or discard at will according to the attitude of men within present circumstances.

Ten years later, the barren Sarah, then about 75, suggested that Abraham sleep with Hagar and **"perhaps,"** said Sarah, **"she can have a child for me."** According to the customs of the neighboring Amorites, Sarah could claim as her own any children Hagar might bear and they would become Abraham's legitimate heirs. Hagar had no say about her role in this matter.

When Hagar became pregnant, she began to think herself better than her mistress who was unable to conceive, and she openly despised her. Sarah became cruel and abusive. Hagar ran away, heading home to Egypt across the arid landscape of Northern Sinai. Why did Sarah not accept the child as her own, according to custom at the time? If Sarah had been a Proverbs 31 woman she would have had kindness on her lips. Her words would not have destroyed or torn down. As women our words should be full of life, hope and restoration. We should always practice a quick smile and the appearance of warmth at a moment's notice.

An angel of God met Hagar at a spring and tenderly told her to **"go back to your mistress. Put up with her abuse. I'm going to give you a big family, children past counting."**

Hagar retraced her steps and gave Abraham, now about

86, his first child, a boy named Ishmael, the name given to Hagar by the angel of God.

Over the next 13 years, there was tension between Sarah and Hagar, especially since Abraham doted on his only son. About the time Ishmael became a teenager, God told Abraham that he would be the ancestor of many nations and that **"the whole land of Canaan will belong to your descendants forever, and I will be their God."** And, said God, Sarah would give birth to a baby boy.

Abraham thought the idea of Sarah, in her 90s, giving birth was silly and besides, he loved Ishmael. **"Why not let Ishmael be my heir?"**

But God said that the agreement would be with Sarah's son. However, **I have heard your request about Ishmael... He will be the father of twelve princes, and I will make a great nation of his descendants."**

Isaac brought Sarah much joy and when he was weaned, Abraham had a great feast, but the celebration went awry. Sarah saw Ishmael making fun and playing with the toddles and went ballistic. She told Abraham to get rid of Hagar and Ishmael because she did not want Ishmael to have any part of Isaac's inheritance. Genesis 21:8-10 Note, she TOLD Abraham, that in itself says she was not obedient to her husband. Women are never to TELL their mates in a demanding tone or give the "look."

This distressed Abraham because Ishmael was his firstborn son, God told him not to feel bad and implied that he would watch over Hagar and Ishmael. And so once again Hagar left Abraham and Sarah, this time with nowhere to go and with only a little food and a leather bag of water. She was driven into the wilderness of Beersheba, with no choice in the matter.

When the food and water were gone, Hagar sat Ishmael under a bush, not wanting to see him die of starvation and began to cry. In her moment of greatest despair, an angel of God came to Hagar again, reiterated God's promise of making a great nation of Ishmael's descendants, and showed her a well.

"God was with the boy as he grew up; he lived in the wilderness of Paran and became a skillful hunter. His mother got an Egyptian wife for him."

Hagar had no say in the events in her life: leaving her family and home in Egypt, bearing Abraham's son, being subjected to harsh treatment by a jealous mistress and being sent to an arid wilderness with her teenage son. However, God sought her out, comforted her and gave her hope for the future. Hagar's life was unfair, but she responded with dignity and faith.

Hagar has been an encouragement to many women who are impoverished, mistreated or enslaved. They hear her story and respond as Hagar did when she first met **"the God who sees me"** - **"Truly have I seen him who looks after me."** Genesis 16:1-16, 17:15-27, 21:1-21

Tamar – Daughter Of King David

Tamar and her brother were the children of Maacah, David's fourth wife, and extraordinarily good looking. Absalom was well known for his good looks and Tamar was very beautiful.

Tamar was young, regal in bearing, a virgin and seemingly innocent of what went on around her. She had the education and training of royalty and was watched over by the Eunuchs who managed the women's quarters in David's palace.

But Amnon, David's oldest son, was inflamed with passion for Tamar, the beautiful virginal half-sister he could not have, so much so that he became sick. The innocent Tamar seemed to be unaware of Amnon's obsession. When Amnon told his streetwise cousin he wanted Tamar, the cousin, knowing the result would be the rape of Tamar, told Amnon to pretend to be ill and to ask David to have Tamar prepare some food and feed it to him.

The ruse worked. Tamar could not refuse her father's request to feed her half-brother. After she cooked some cakes for him, Amnon ordered everyone else to leave. Then he told Tamar he wanted her to feed him in private, in his bedroom. Once they were alone, he grabbed her and told her to come to bed with him. Struggling for her virginity, her reputation and even her life, Tamar response showed her character and innocence.

"No, brother! Don't hurt me! This kind of thing isn't done in Israel! Don't do this terrible thing! Where could I ever show my face? And you; you'll be out on the street in disgrace. Oh, please! Speak to the King. He'll let you marry me."

Amnon didn't care what Tamar said. He raped her. He violated her. He ruined her life. But he was not done. After he had gotten what he wanted, he began to feel a hated greater than the passion he had had for her. **"Get up and get out."**

"Oh no, brother. Please! This is a even worse evil than what you just did to me!"

Tamar knew that she could never marry or have children. She would be unwanted, an outcast. Within a few minutes, all her hopes and dreams had been shattered.

Amnon despised her and called his valet, who threw Tamar out of the house and locked the door behind her. But the insults were not over.

Sobbing, Tamar took some of the cooling ashes from the cooking fire and put them on her head. She tore her beautiful robe, and staggered through the palace weeping. When her brother, Absalom, found out, he did what so many people have done when confronted with violence against a woman. He minimized it.

"Has your brother Amnon had his way with you? Now, my dear sister, let's keep it quiet; a family matter. He is, after all, your bother. Don't take this so hard."

When David heard about Amnon's rape of Tamar, he

was furious. But Amnon was David's firstborn. He had grown up getting whatever he wanted from his doting father. David did not punish Amnon. He protected the abuser rather than the victim. And when the King did not take action, others were powerless to help Tamar. She moved into Absalom's house, where she lived out her life as a desolate woman, having been wronged by Amnon, Absalom and her father, David. That's the last we know of her. She was never given the opportunity to become a Proverbs 31 woman, which is extremely sad.

Two years later, Absalom invited all his brothers to a banquet and killed Amnon. When David heard about it, he thought all of his sons had been killed, but the double-crossing streetwise cousin told him it was not a big deal, **"for Amnon alone is dead,"** indicating that the cousin had been in on the plot to kill Amnon for carrying out the plan the cousin had suggested to him.
11 Samuel 13:1-33

Leah

Very seldom does the Bible tell us what women feel, think, or say. The silence of women makes Leah's few words, each time she bears a son, poignant and heartbreaking. This is the time for Leah's perspective.

After Jacob had stolen Isaac's blessing from his brother Esau, Rebekah told him to stay with her brother, Laban, until Esau **"forgets what you have done to him."** Did Rebekah take any responsibility for her part in the deception?

When Jacob arrived at a well near where Laban lived, Rachel (Laban's younger daughter and Jacob's cousin) approached with a flock of sheep. Rachel was "shapely and beautiful" and Jacob fell in love at once. He told Laban what happened back in Canaan, and Laban let Jacob stay with the family.

Laban offered to pay Jacob to work for him and Jacob said he'd work for Laban for seven years in exchange for

Rachel's hand in marriage. If the fortune Jacob took with him when he fled from Esau after deceiving his Father Isaac, would not have become lost, it might have been Jacob and Rachel marrying and living happily ever after. But it did not work that way.

Laban's older daughter, Leah, had "weak eyes," whatever that means. Commentators have been trying to figure it out for 3,000 years; the writer of Genesis contrasted it with Rachel's stunning beauty. Whether Jacob was attracted to Rachel's mind, personality or body, he was passionately in love with her, NOT Leah.

At the end of the seven years, Laban hosted a big marriage feast and when evening came, Jacob slept with his veiled bride in the marriage bed. In the morning, Jacob realized he had married Leah, not Rachel. Jacob was understandably upset that Laban had deceived him. **"Why have you tricked me?"**

"It is not the custom here to give the younger daughter in marriage celebrations before the older," said Laban. **"Wait until the week's marriage celebrations are over, and I will give you Rachel, if you will work for me another seven-years." Laban and Leah should have been forthright and honest and given Jacob a choice. I believe Jacob would have made the right choice. Instead he did right and fulfilled the wedding week even though he had been deceived (as he deceived his Father years earlier) and then was given Rachel in exchange for another seven years work. Apparently Leah did not have a spontaneous sparkling personality. She also may not have been skilled in relationships and had no suitors. Leah was a follow-through person. She gave birth to many children and no complaints hoping each time that Jacob would "really" love her as he loved Rachel. Did it happen? We do not know because Scripture does not tell us. Did she and Rachel fight? Probably. I do believe that either one of them were a "pushover" even though they were deceived.**

Both women were committed to the success of their families. Did their children rise up and call them blessed, probably. Did their husband Jacob, praise them also. Probably. At least, let's hope he did. And let's hope above all else, that Jacob honored the God of Abraham and Isaac the rest of his days.

But focus on Leah instead of Jacob and Rachel. Leah's fate was not her own to decide. There is no indication that she had other suitors, but on the night of her wedding, she knew that the love expressed by her husband was not for her. The Bible makes it crystal clear: Jacob **"loved Rachel more than Leah."**

It also says that Leah was hated, perhaps by her father who saw her as a way of getting seven more years of work out of Jacob, perhaps by her sister Rachel who wanted to hold the place of honor as Jacob first wife, and certainly by her husband who had been tricked into marrying her. Leah had been dealt a bad hand and was desperate for love, respect and affection. God opened her womb and over time she bore six sons and one daughter.

With the birth of each son, she explained why she chose each name. The agony on Leah's soul is revealed in her explanations:

- **Reuben,** meaning "a son": "The Lord has seen my trouble, and now my husband will love me."
- **Simeon,** meaning "hear": "The Lord has given me this son also, because he heard that I was not loved."
- **Levi,** meaning "bound": "Now my husband will be bound more tightly to me, because I have borne him three sons."
- **Judah,** meaning "praise": "This time I will praise the Lord."

More than likely Leah may have worshipped pagan gods

because her father had many pagan gods he worshipped. She was not an Israelite, but a Gentile. At the birth of Judah, Leah's focus turned from her husband to God.

The still-barren Rachel, jealous of her sister, blamed Jacob: **"Give me children, or I will die!"** She told him he should sleep with her maid, Bilhah. Bilhah bore two sons.

One can only imagine how routine was Jacob's sex with Leah. It was his duty, and no more. One day, Leah's son Reuben found some mandrakes, a plant with narcotic qualities and considered a love potion, and brought them to his mother. Rachel wanted some. Leah burst out, **"Wasn't it enough that you got my husband away from me? And now you also want my son's mandrakes?"** As you can tell, the tension between these sisters was great and very soulful. There were a lot of challenges between them. One bore children when the other did not. The one whom bore children really wanted just to be loved. The other was loved but couldn't bring forth children at that time and was frustrated because of it. Maybe you can feel all this tension between these two sisters. Sometimes it was pointed at each other. Sometimes the guilt was inward and so deep she might have felt there is no way out. The guilt of being married first... (Leah) maybe conspring with her father so she could finally have a man. Did she REALLY have a choice in the matter? Maybe Laban forced Leah to marry Jacob. She might have come to terms with what she thought all along... that Jacob was not hers from the very beginning. Was it worth the chance of being married and having a man who doesn't really want you verses not being married and hoping that one day the man who will love you shows up? Could part of the division between the two sisters been caused because Leah wanted what she wanted? When you look at all the scenarios that are possible, it can make for one very depressed lady. While rarely stated, many women can relate to Leah at many levels. The bottom line, she didn't understand. And that gives us hope.

Mandrakes and Fertility Rites – Fertility was valued throughout the ancient Middle East, but among the covenant people it had only one true source: the Lord. In the Book of Genesis, Abraham speaks of "the children whom God has graciously given. Genesis 33:5. "Although all children, sons and daughters, were acknowledged as God's gifts, in a patrilineal society sons were especially prized. Psalm 127 compares sons to "arrows in the hand of a warrior... Happy is the man who has his quiver full of them." If a woman was barren, her recourse was to petition God to remove the curse that he had placed upon her.

However, fertility lore abounded, and there were many remedies to tempt the desperate. The mandrake plant, in particular, was thought to have properties that aroused desire and stimulated conception. In Genesis, Leah and Rachel evidently believed in the mandrake's power and quarreled over possession of mandrake roots that Leah's son found, but it is clear that God alone enabled the two women to have children by Jacob. In the Song of Solomon, a maiden enticed her lover with the fragrance of mandrakes.

The Israelites were not always successful in resisting the fertility myths and rituals of the Babylonians, Canaanites, Egyptians, and other ancient peoples. Kings of Israel, including Solomon, Omri, and Ahab, and Kings of Judah, such as Rehoboam, Jehoram, Ahaziah, and Manasseh, erected shrines to fertility deities. Such apostasy outraged prophets like Jeremiah, who berated Hebrew women for making offerings to a "queen of heaven." Jeremiah 7:18 She was in fact, an alien goddess. (A number of clay figurines of pregnant women, perhaps statues dedicated to a fertility goddess, have been unearthed at archeological sites in Israel.

Outside influences challenged but did not break the belief that the true giver of all life was the God of Israel, whose blessings were not obtained by fertility rites but by obedience to his law. **"If you obey the voice of the Lord,"** the Torah promises, **"blessed shall be the fruit of your** body, and the fruit of your ground, the increase of your cattle, and the young of your flock.** Deuteronomy 28:2

Over the mandrakes, Rachel's reply is stunningly revealing. **"I'll let Jacob sleep with you tonight."**

And when Jacob came home, his own wife had the humiliation of saying to him, **"Sleep with me tonight; I've bartered my son's mandrakes for a night with you."**

Although she had sons, Leah followed Rachel's example by giving Jacob her maid, Zilpah, who bore two sons. Leah herself then had two more boys and her focus turned back to her longing for her husband's love, approval and comfort:

> ➢ **Issachar**, meaning "there is reward": "God has given me my reward, because I gave my slave to my husband."
> ➢ **Zebulun**, meaning "accept": "God has given me a fine gift. Now my husband will accept me, because I have bone him six sons."

Rachel eventually gave birth to Joseph. She then died in childbirth with Benjamin and was buried on the outskirts of Bethlehem.

Perhaps after Rachel's death Jacob turned his love and attention to Leah, for when she died, Jacob gave Leah the honor of burial in the family tomb along with Abraham, Sarah, Isaac and Rebekah. And just before he died, Jacob requested that he too might be buried there, next to Leah, the wife who longed for his love.
Genesis 29:1-30:24, 49:29-33

Woman Whom Solomon Loved

Abishag

The story of Abishag does not make it into many Bible storybooks. When King David was so old and bedridden that he could not get warm no matter how many blankets were put over him, his servants searched for the most ravishingly good-looking girl they could find to be the King's bed warmer. **"She will lie close to you and keep you warm,"** they said to David.

The girl was Abishag. The plan did not work. The King did not have sex with her as he was unable. Abishag was young and very beautiful. David was old, bedridden, possibly incontinent and slowly dying, hardly the man of Abishag's dreams. And yet she became his perfect helper. She looked after the King's every need. Obviously, she had great compassion. When Bathsheba went to see David about who would be the next King, Abishag was at his side making sure he was comfortable.

Later Abishag became a pawn in court politics when David's son Adonijah tried to have her given to him as his wife as part of a plot to secure the throne.

It is believed in Jewish culture that she was the Shulmite Bride in Song of Solomon and that Solomon loved her very much. Did she have the opportunity to become a Proverbs 31 woman? Scripture does not tell us, but we know that she was kind and not lazy. Being a caregiver is difficult at best, but obedience to God is the greater value. She was the one woman Solomon had in his life, he found a pearl of great price.

1 Kings 1:1-4, 1:15, 2:13-24

The Woman In The House Of Simon The Pharisee

Simon, a Pharisee, invited Jesus to his home for dinner. He probably wanted to know more about this teacher who had been healing people and teaching in synagogues. He was concerned because Jesus did not seem to understand that a pious Jew should separate himself from those who neglected the Law of God. Simon had even heard that Jesus was a glutton and wine drinker and a friend of tax collectors and other outcasts! He wanted to see Jesus for himself.

When Jesus arrived at Simon's house, he greeted the

other guests and reclined at the dinner table. Jews and Romans ate dinner leaning on their elbows, propped up on a cushion, with their feet stretched out behind them.

Things were going well until an uninvited woman walked in and stood at Jesus' feet. Simon thought, **"If this man really were a prophet, he would know who this woman is who is touching him; he would know what kind of sinful life she lives!"** Luke 7:39 Simon saw this woman as damaged goods. And by the rules he lived by, she certainly was unclean. If a leper or sinner touched a good Jew, the Jew became unclean. Simon's world revolved around being separate, staying ceremonially clean and maintaining his status and reputation. This uninvited guest, however, had evidently heard Jesus' message of forgiveness for sinners.

Impulsively, she did what no woman should do in public. She let down her hair, a sign of sexual promiscuity. On a wedding night a bride would let down her hair, showing it to her husband for the first time. Standing at Jesus' feet, the woman was overcome with emotion, and wept. She held his feet tenderly and washed them with her tears, dried them with her hair and kissed them. She had brought an alabaster jar of expensive perfume that she poured on his feet.

The Bible does not say that she was a prostitute, but she was known to be a sinner and used the tools of her presumed trade (her touch, her hair, her kisses, her perfume) to worship Jesus. Every man secretly wishes for a Proverbs 31 woman in his life. Few can qualify for her. Proverbs 18:22 says "Whoso findeth a wife findeth a good thing and obtaineth favor of the LORD." I am certain that those men's hearts longed for the kind of attention she lavished on Jesus. The honey of the "soul".

Simon, a respected citizen, a leader in his synagogue and a good man, was horrified by this excessive public display of affection. It made him and his guests uncomfortable. Jesus, however, received the woman's actions warmly. He had no problem with this sinner making him ceremonially unclean.

Knowing what Simon was thinking. Jesus told a parable about two men who owed money. One owed 500 coins and the other 50. The moneylender canceled both their debts. Jesus asked, **Which one will love him more?" Luke 7:42** Simon answered cautiously, **"I suppose that it would be the one who was forgiven more."** Luke 7:43 Jesus continued, aggressively defending the woman's actions. **"Do you see this woman? I came into your home, and you gave me no water for my feet, but she has washed my feet with her tears and dried them with her hair. You did not welcome me with a kiss, but she has not stopped kissing my feet since I came. You provided no olive oil for my head, but she has covered my feet with perfume. I tell you, then, the great love she has shown proves that her many sins have been forgiven. But whoever has been forgiven little shows only a little love." Luke 7:44-47** Turning to the woman, Jesus did not shame her, reject her or condemn her. He accepted her love for him and said, **"Your sins are forgiven. Your faith has saved you; go in peace." Luke 7:48**

Women Whom Met Jesus And Loved

Mary and Martha

They were two unmarried sisters who lived in the quiet village of Bethany with their brother, Lazarus, just over the hill from downtown Jerusalem. Scripture does not tell us how they meet, but Jesus loved this family and he frequently visited in their home. It was unusual for all three siblings to be unmarried, so they may have been orphaned, fairly well-off and young, perhaps in their 20's or even late teens. They were certainly Proverbs 31 women to their brother, to Jesus and his disciples. Here are listed some concepts of a virtuous woman which need to be discussed, understood and put into practice. She does exist. She simply must be found. She is among thousands, not average. She is not common or normal.

She is not easily discovered. What the average woman will do, she REFUSES to do. What the average woman will wear, she REFUSES to wear. She does not even respond to the same kind of man the average woman responds to. What makes an average woman angry, makes her THOUGHTFUL. What makes an average woman bitter, makes her SWEET. Her THOUGHTS are different. And her CONDUCT AND BEHAVIOR are different.

Mary and Martha had distinctly different personalities. Martha was organized, ran the household, helped other people and was practical. Mary was creative, less stressed, more reflective, less concerned about schedules. Theologians and thinkers have distinguished between the active life (how most of us live) and the contemplative life (how monks live, spending most of their time in prayer and meditation). Martha was held up as a example of the active life while Mary was held up as an example of the contemplative life.

Mary and Martha appear three times in the Renewed Testament. The first vignette shows the difference in their personalities. Jesus and his disciples were on their way to Jerusalem and stopped at Bethany, where Martha **"welcomed them into her home."** While Martha was making dinner, Mary sat by Jesus, listening to his teaching. Martha told Jesus she needed Mary to lend her a hand, but Jesus seemed to say the contemplative life was more important than the active life. "Martha, dear Martha, you're fussing far too much and getting yourself worked up over nothing. One thing only is essential, and Mary has chosen it."

In the second vignette, Lazarus became sick and the sisters sent word to Jesus, expecting him to heal their brother, but Lazarus died before Jesus got to Bethany. Martha went out to meet Jesus, telling him if he had come sooner Lazarus would not have died. They even had a bit of a theological discussion and Martha said she believed Jesus was the Messiah, the Son of God.

Mary, reacting in her own way, ran outside, fell at his

feet weeping, and also said that if Jesus had been here Lazarus would not have died. When Jesus ordered the stone to be moved from Lazarus' tomb, Martha made the practical observation that there would be a bad smell because Lazarus had been buried four days. **"Lazarus, come out!"** Jesus said, Lazarus did, and many people believed in Jesus upon hearing about it. The Jewish culture did not believe that one was deceased until after four days, that is why Jesus delayed his return to Bethany. On the fourth day any one was declared DEAD.

The third vignette took place a few days later and, again, the two sisters exhibited their different personality types. Martha had prepared a dinner for Jesus and his friends at the home of Simon, the leper. While Jesus was at the table, in what seemed much like a re-enactment of the experience in the home of Simon the Pharisee, Mary poured perfume on him. Judas, one of the disciples, complained because Mary had wasted an entire jar of perfume on Jesus. The expensive perfume cost as much as a laborer's wages for a year.

Jesus said, **"Leave her alone! Why are you bothering her? She has done a fine and beautiful thing for me... I assure you that where ever the gospel is preached all over the world, what she has done will be told in memory of her."**
Luke 10:38-42, John 11:1-46, Matthew 26:6-13; Mark 14:3-9, John 12:1-8

The Samaritan Woman At The Well

There appear to be three good reasons why Jesus should not have said, "Give me a drink of water." The person he spoke to was a Samaritan, (half Jewish and half Gentile or Assyrian) she was an outcast woman and drinking from her cup would make him unclean. She would not have been a Proverbs 31 woman because she had multiple husbands AND the one she lived with she was not married to. After meeting

Jesus she may have become one?

The Samaritans and Jews did not get along. The Samaritans were as stated above half-Jewish and half-Assyrian people living between Jerusalem and Galilee, and they had a long history of bitter hostility with the Jews. The Samaritans arrogantly regarded themselves as the only true Jews. The Jews had a magnificent Temple in Jerusalem, the Samaritans had had a magnificent Temple on Mount Gerizim, at least they did until a Jewish Maccabean leader destroyed it about 150 years earlier. The Jews called the Samaritans "that foolish people" and the Samaritans considered Jews apostates (people who abandon their faith). The most direct route from Jerusalem to Galilee was through Samaria, but most Jews would take a longer route just to avoid Samaritans.

A Hebrew man did not talk with women in the street, which is why the disciples, upon returning from a trip to Sychar for food, were **"greatly surprised to find Jesus talking with a woman."** This woman was an outcast who had had a hard life. She was not married to the man she was living with. She had gone to the well at the hottest time of the day when others were not there so she would not have to experience their critical looks.

It was against the ceremonial laws of the Jews for Jesus to drink from an unclean cup belonging to a sinful person. Touching the cup or the woman would make Jesus ceremonially unclean. But Jesus did ask this woman for a drink, and, in one fell swoop, he broke racial, gender and religious taboos.

The dialog between Jesus and the outcast Samaritan woman is his longest recorded conversation with anyone, and one of the most profound. In it he made three important statements.

1. About the woman.
"You are right when you say you don't have a

husband. You have been married to five men, and the man you live with now is not really your husband."
2. About God.
   "God is Spirit, and only by the power of his Spirit can people worship him as he really is."
3. About himself.
   After the woman said, **"I know that the Messiah will come,** Jesus said, **"I am he."** It was the first time he had explicitly and clearly unveiled his true identity as the Messiah. (Could John 9:35-41 be another time Yeshua revealed He was the Messiah?)

After this, the woman took off for Sychar where she told everyone what she saw and heard, **"Come and see the man who told me everything I have ever done. Could he be the Messiah?"** Many Samaritans, people who were despised and looked down upon by the Jews, believed in Jesus because of what the woman told them.

It's quite a contrast to the one other time Jesus explicitly said he was the Messiah. At Jesus' trial the High Priest asked him directly if he were the Messiah. Jesus said, **"I am."** The High Priest tore his robes, shouted, **"Blasphemy,"** and voted to put Jesus to death.

Jesus stayed in Sychar for two days and many more believed **"because we ourselves have heard him, and we know that he really is the Saviour of the world."**
John 4:3-42

The Woman Caught In The Act Of Adultery

And with what judgment you judge, you will be judged; and with the measure you use, it will be measured back to you. And why do you look at the speck in your brother's eye, but do not consider the plank in your own eye? Or how can you say to your brother. **"Let me remove the speck from** your eye; and look, a plank is in your own eye? Hypocrite! First remove the plank from your own eye, and then you will see clearly to remove the speck from your brothers eye."** Jesus in the Sermon on the Mount.

Jesus was teaching in the Temple in Jerusalem. Many believed him, but the religious officials called Pharisees were so upset with his teaching that they sent the Temple police to arrest him. The police came back empty-handed because, they said they could not arrest a person who taught as Jesus did.

Early the next morning, Jesus returned to the Temple and people gathered around to hear him. Some Pharisees brought to him a woman "caught right in the act of adultery." Jesus stopped teaching. Everyone watched. The atmosphere was tense. The Pharisees said, **"Moses, in the Law, gives orders to stone such persons. What do you say?"**

Both the woman and Jesus knew they were being set up. If the Pharisees really wanted to see the law observed, they would have brought the man as well as the woman. She would not committing adultery by herself, and the Law of Moses said both the man and woman should be put to death. If Jesus did not condemn the woman, he would appear to be ignoring the Law of Moses. If he said she should be stoned, he would violate Roman law. He would lose either way.

The situation this woman encountered is far more common than we might want to acknowledge. The treatment of her was callous and demeaning. She had no opportunity to speak for herself. Everyone around her except Jesus was indifferent to her suffering. Accusations? Let ones words be sweet and tender for tomorrow we may have to eat them.

To the Pharisees, she was not a person, but a thing, a prop heartlessly used in their desire to trick Jesus. To the crowd, she was an object to scorn. Now these good people at the Temple would all know she was a sinner. To herself, she realized life was not fair. She could expect a brutal and violent death while her lover was let go.

Jesus said nothing. He began writing in the dirt, only it was the Temple floor, not dirt (10 And the LORD delivered unto me two tables of stone written with the finger of God; and on them *was written* according to all the words, which the LORD spake with you in the mount out of the midst of the fire in the day of the assembly. Deuteronomy 9:10. Do you see the connection?). The Pharisees kept after him. He said, **"The sinless one among you, go first. Throw the stone."** No longer was the woman an **"it."** Jesus made it personal. Which of the Pharisees was without sin and was willing by his own hand to cause this woman's death? In Torah it states when a witness or accuser must be the first one to, in this case, throw the first stone so she dies by being stoned to death. The hands of the witnesses shall be first upon him to put him to death, and afterward the hands of all the people. So thou shalt put the evil away from among you. Deuteronomy 17:7

The Pharisees were under the watchful eye of all those who had been listening to Jesus teach. One by one the Pharisees walked away.

"Woman," Jesus asked, **"Where are they" Does no one condemn you?"**

"No one, Master."

"Neither do I. Go on your way. From now on don't sin."

Jesus treated her like a person, not a thing. He took away her scorn in front of the crowd watching at the Temple. He gave her a second chance. He is the God of restoration.
John 8:2-11

Women At The Tomb Of Jesus

The Apostle Paul said about the Christian faith, "If there's no resurrection for Christ, everything we've told you is smoke and mirrors, and everything you've staked your life on is smoke and mirrors. The resurrection of Jesus Christ from the dead is a pivotal event in the history of Christianity. The first people to find out about the Resurrection were four women: Mary Magdalene; Joanna; Mary, the mother of James and Joses; and Salome. It was they who were charged with telling the disciples that Jesus had risen from the dead.

Mary Magdalene

She is one of the best known and most misunderstood women in the Renewed Covenant (New Testament). Although Mary was an important follower of Jesus Christ, she is mentioned only once in the Renewed Testament until near the end of Jesus' life. There she plays a more prominent role at Jesus' death, burial, Resurrection and post-Resurrection appearances than any of his followers, even more so than the disciples. I am certain to Jesus and the disciples, women, and children in their group she was more than a Proverbs 31 woman. It is NORMAL to desire security. It is NORMAL to desire to be under the covering of a successful man. Why? Men are realistic and women are emotional. It takes more than money to get the attention and time of a true Proverbs 31 woman. Why? She is financially competent herself. She is comfortable with money. She can transact business. Only a foolish and immature man would attempt to impress or control her with his money. She trusted and loved Jesus, it was that simple. She was not a burden to him. She never distracted his focus. She never embarrassed him. She knew the greatness in him and she never pulled him backward away from his dreams or future. She was consistent and very loyal.

Mary was from Magdala, an important fishing village on the northwest coast of the Sea of Galilee, not far from Capernaum. She was one of three named women, along with others, who traveled with Jesus and **"who used their own resources to help Jesus and his disciples."** She may have inherited some money or been a widow. She was an independent and well-to-do woman who could control her own money and spend time with Jesus. She was totally dedicated to Him.

Jesus had driven seven demons from Mary. Sometimes "having a demon" in the Renewed Testament may have indicated a severe illness, at other times, it seems to indicate the person was tormented by demon possession. We do not know details about Mary's demons, but we do know Jesus had healed her.

Mary is mentioned, along with several other women and John, as being at the Crucifixion of Jesus, **"looking on from a distance."** Other followers had probably fled because it was dangerous to show sympathy for a person being crucified. Sometimes people who wept in public at the execution of a friend or relative were themselves executed. The followers of Jesus were afraid.

When Jesus was removed from the tree (cross), Joseph, a man from a town Northwest of Jerusalem, asked for the body, wrapped it in linen and put it in a cave used as a tomb. Mary Magdalene and Mary, the mother of James and Joses, watched while Jesus was buried. The burial took place and on Sabbath at 3 in the afternoon (Matthew 27:46), on the 7th day Jesus was resurrected. No work was to be done on Sabbath. Mary Magdalene, found Him in the garden and she was weeping. He tenderly said, "Mary" she realized it was the resurrected Jesus and her grief turned to JOY. He instructed her not to touch him because he had not yet ascended unto the Father. She ran and told the disciples, which did not believe her. So Peter and John ran to see for themselves, and Mary Magdalene went with them. They found that she was correct.

Then later, the women went with Mary Magdalene, with Mary, the mother of James and Joses, Joanna, and Salome, whom had waited until the Sabbath was over to take spices to the tomb to anoint Jesus' body. They did not know how they would get inside, but Mary Magdalene already knew for He had risen and the tomb was empty.

Mary Magdalene's importance is that she said to the disciples, **"I have seen the Lord."** As stated above Mary was one of the four women who first learned that Jesus has been raised from the dead. Mary Magdalene was the first to talk to the resurrected Jesus and she was the person who told the disciples that Jesus had risen. Her witness to the most important event for all Christians is the reason she has been called the Apostle to the Apostles.

Joanna

She was born into a prominent and wealthy Jewish family from Galilee. Her parents arranged her marriage to Chuza, a young man from what is now Jordon and Saudi Arabia. Chuza rose through the ranks to become finance minister of Herod's kingdom.

Joanna and Chuza lived in a magnificent house in Tiberias, a city that Herod had recently built as his Capital. There were aspirations that Tiberias would be a Roman city in culture and style, much to the irritation and resentment of the Jews who lived around it in Galilee. Joanna was more independent than the average Jewish woman because she lived a Roman lifestyle and had her own wealth, given to her by her father when she married.

Perhaps it was the extraordinary stories of Jesus' healing power, or perhaps Joanna herself was healed by Jesus, but she became one of his followers and it changed her life. She knew that the healings Jesus performed were related to his vision of the coming Kingdom of God. For those who followed him, this included a call to repentance, a decision to let God's forgiveness transform their lives and membership in a group that included many on the margins of society: beggars, prostitutes and outcasts.

It was particularly difficult for Joanna that the followers of Jesus renounced all status and wealth. The conspicuous wealth of Tiberias determined her lifestyle, but she turned her back on it to join the rag-tag band of followers of Jesus. She even helped support them with substantial donations to the common fund. Most of the male disciples had left wives and children at home and had nothing to spare.

For two years she followed Jesus all over Israel. Sometimes as many as one hundred followed him, sometimes fewer. The most consistent followers were his twelve disciples and a group of women including Joanna and Mary Magdalene. They listened to him teach and watched him heal and sometimes the disciples were sent out in pairs to visit towns and villages preaching about the Kingdom of God.

When Jesus arrived in Jerusalem the last time, Joanna still had connections in high places and was one of the first to hear that he had been sentenced to die by crucifixion. With much courage, she watched Jesus' agonizing death. After he Sabbath was over, she was among the four women who took spices and ointments to his tomb to anoint his body. These four were the first to hear **"He is not here; he has been raised."** They ran and told the disciples the miraculous story that Joanna would repeat a thousand times the rest of her life.

Because of his position in Herod's court, Joanna's husband, Chuza, had to be careful of talking too much about his wife's association with Jesus. He was in Jerusalem for the Passover when Jesus was crucified and was deeply disturbed by his death. He was with Joanna and many other followers when Jesus appeared to them and told them to **"go, then, to all the peoples everywhere and make them my disciples."**

Joanna and Chuza became raveling missionaries through out Palestine. Eventually they were asked to go to Rome because they knew a little Latin and were familiar with Roman culture, having lived in Tiberias. Joanna began using the Latin equivalent of her name, Junia, and Chuza adopted the Greek name Andronicus. Ten years later, when Paul wrote to the Christians in Rome, he told them to **"greet Andronicus and Junia. They are well known to the apostles, and they were in Christ before me."**

Luke 8:1-2, 24:1-10, Romans 16:7

Mary – Mother Of James And Joses.
The name of Mary was used more often than people think in the Renewed Covenant. Frankly, it can be confusing. The four gospels speak of a Mary who was at the cross, at the burial of Jesus and at the tomb. There are several names used that are all the same person: Mary, the mother of Jesus; Mary, the mother of James, Jesus Brother; Mary, the mother of James; Mary, mother of James and Joses; Mary, mother of James the Less and of Joses; Mary, mother of James and Joseph; Mary, mother of Joses; the other Mary; and Mary, wife of Clopas. To add to the confusion, Clopas was probably the same person as Alphaeus, and so Mary's two sons were James, son of Alphaeus, and Joses.

James, son of Alphaeus, was one of the 12 disciples, and both he and his mother, Mary, followed Jesus in Galilee, throughout Israel and went to Jerusalem with him. This Mary was one of the four women who stayed by Jesus at the cross, watched his burial and went to the tomb. Undoubtedly she was also with the disciples when the risen Jesus first appeared to them.
Matthew 27:55-61, 28:1-8; Luke 24:1-10, John 19:25-27

Salome
The Bible says nothing about Salome except that she was a follower of Jesus who was present at his Crucifixion and was one of the four women at the tomb who were told that Jesus had risen from the dead. In apocryphal writings and tradition, she is sometimes said to be the wife of Zebedee and, therefore, the mother of James and John, two of the 12 disciples. She is also sometimes said to be the sister of Mary, the mother of Jesus.
Mark 15:40-41, 16:1-8

The Mother of Jesus

When Mary arrived at Elizabeth's home, both Elizabeth and the baby in her womb were overjoyed upon hearing that God had promised Mary she would give birth to the Messiah. Mary then gave praise to God in a psalm or prayer that is reminiscent of Hannah's prayer when she took the child Samuel to Eli the priest. Mary's song, called "The Magnificent" (the first word in its Latin version). My soul doth magnify the Lord and my spirit hath rejoiced in God my Saviour. For he hath regarded the lowliness of his hand maiden. For behold, from henceforth all generations shall call me blessed. For he that is mighty hath magnified me and holy is his Name. And his mercy is on them that fear him throughout all generations. He hath shewed strength with his arm he hath scattered the proud in the imagination of their hearts. He hath filled the hungry with good things and the rich he hath sent empty away. He remembering his mercy hath helped his servant Israel as he promised to our forefathers, Abraham and his seed forever.

--

The amazing thing about the women in the life of Jesus is that there were so many. Jesus lived in a patriarchal society in which women's rights were restricted. With a few exceptions, women could not inherit property, the word of a woman was not permitted as witness in a legal matter, and women were not worthy to be taught the Scripture. But Jesus treated women and men without distinction. He addressed each woman as a person and did not disgrace, belittle, reproach or stereotype anyone, even men.

Jesus accepted and respected women and seemed to have no problem with scandalous encounters. It was scandalous for Jesus to talk with a Samaritan woman. It was scandalous to allow Mary of Bethany to sit at his feet and listen to his teaching. It was scandalous to permit the woman in Simon the Pharisee's house to kiss his feet, wash them with her tears, and wipe them with her hair.

The story of Jesus begins with a woman, his mother

Mary and his step-father, Joseph and ends with a group of women. Except for John, the only followers who stayed with Jesus at the cross were women. Mary Mageadalen who was then told to tell the others. Women were important in the life of Jesus.

--

Elizabeth

The Bible was written entirely by men through the inspiration of the Holy Spirit. Luke, who wrote both the gospel named for him as well as the Acts of the Apostles, was a physician. Perhaps it was his medical background that helped him to write so knowingly about Elizabeth's experience when she was six months pregnant.

Elizabeth was the wife of a Jewish priest, Zaharias, who worked in the Temple in Jerusalem where her father, who had also been a priest, might have worked. Elizabeth and her husband took their faith and its practice seriously and served their God well. They were both old and had no children because Elizabeth was barren. Zacharias must have loved her because her childlessness could have been grounds for divorce.

One day the angel Gabriel appeared to Zacharias in the Temple and told him that Elizabeth would have a son, who should be named John. "John will be great in the Lord's sight," said Gabriel. **"From his very birth he will be filled with the Holy Spirit. He will bring fathers and children together again; he will turn disobedient people back to the way of thinking of the righteous; he will get the Lord's people ready for him."**

Like Abraham when God told him his wife Sarah would have a child in her old age, Zacharias did not believe the angel because he and Elizabeth were well advanced in years. Because he did not believe the angel, he was struck dumb. **"You will remain silent until the day my promise to you comes true,"** said Gabriel.

The angel's words did come true and Elizabeth became

pregnant. **"The Lord has taken away my public disgrace!"** she said.

Gabriel was busy that year. Six months after visiting Zacharias, he told Mary, a relative of Elizabeth, that Mary would become pregnant, that she was highly favored. The angel then told Joseph that it was alright to take Mary as his wife as she was carrying the Son of God, Yeshua.

As soon as Mary walked into the house and greeted Elizabeth, **""the baby in Elizabeth's womb leaped. She was filled with the Holy Spirit, and sang out exuberantly. You're so blessed among women, and the babe in your womb, also blessed! And why am I so blessed that the mother of my Lord visits me? The moment the sound of your greeting entered my ears, the babe in my womb skipped like a lamb for sheet joy."** The movement of the fetus in Elizabeth's womb confirmed the blessing of God and the truth of his promise.

Mary went to Elizabeth's to escape her community wanting to stone her to death, because they could not find the man, because the child's Father was God. She was the daughter of a priest and her pregnancy would have been enough to have her burned or stoned according to Torah. Leviticus 21:9 - **"And the daughter of any priest, if she profane herself by playing he harlot, (pregnancy) she profaneth her far father: she shall be burned with fire."**

Shortly after Mary went back to Nazareth to join her husband, Elizabeth gave birth to John. All her friends and neighbors assumed the child's name would be Zacharias, after his father. But Elizabeth said it would be **"John"**, which did not make any sense according to Jewish custom.

They then asked Zacharias, who wrote, **"His name is John."** Zacharias, silenced earlier by the angel Gabriel, was immediately able to speak and said, **"You, my child, will be called a prophet of the Most High God. You will go ahead of the Lord to prepare his road for him, to tell his people that they will be saved by having their sins forgiven."**

Within months of one another, Elizabeth and Mary had both become pregnant by miraculous means and given birth to sons who were great in the Lord's sight. And both sons would experience violent deaths. Elizabeth's son would be beheaded by Herod Antipas and Mary's, the Son of God would be crucified.
Luke 1:5-80

Mary, The Mother Of Jesus
 She who gave birth to Jesus Christ is the most honored, revered and influential woman in the world. Magnificent cathedrals have been built in her name. Women and men have dedicated their lives in religious orders devoted to her. She has been the central figure in art, novels, music and plays. Millions of pilgrims today visit shrines where she is said to have appeared. But the facts are she is just as sinful as we are and her Son came to save her also. Her story in the Scriptures is simple and well known. The story of her adoration after the death of her Son is longer and much more complicated.
 Mary stood out above all other women as the most blessed, the most highly favored by God. After Mary learned that she would give birth to Jesus, she said, **"from now on all generations will call me blessed; for he who is mighty has done great things for me and holy is his name." She is to be honored, emulated, and remembered.**
 Mary grew up in Nazareth, an unimportant little town West of the Sea of Galilee and about 70 miles North of Jerusalem. When Philip told Nathanael about **"Jesus of Nazareth"** Nathanael sneered, **"Can anything good come from Nazareth?"** The people of Nazareth never did believe in the teachings of Jesus. In fact, they almost threw him off a cliff once. When we first meet Mary, she is quite young, perhaps a teenager. She had a sister, was related to Elizabeth, was promised in marriage to Joseph, and was a descendant of King David. That's all the Bible says about her background.

When Elizabeth had been pregnant for six months, the angel Gabriel appeared to Mary and told her that she would have a son. **"You will name him Jesus. He will be great and will be called the Son of the Most High God."**
Mary was skeptical. **"I am a virgin. How, then, can this be?"** The angel told her she would conceive by the power of the Holy Spirit without the help of a human Father. **"I am the Lord's servant,"** said Mary; **"may it happen to me as you have said."**
When she told Joseph, he was skeptical too; but his concern was about Mary's faithfulness to him; and, not wanting to disgrace her, made plans to break off the engagement as quietly as possible. The angel Gabriel then told Joseph that Mary had conceived by the Holy Spirit, and so Joseph and Mary married without waiting for the end of their engagement period. Mary went to Elizabeth's house near Jerusalem where she spent three months (explained prior) perhaps to minimize the gossip in Nazareth and save hers and the child's life, as the young girl who had become pregnant before getting married.

The stories surrounding the birth of Jesus are repeated most every feast day and are very familiar. Mary and Joseph went to Bethlehem because of a census. They could not find a room and so they went to "The Tower of the Sheep" where she gave birth and laid the baby in a ceremonial clean manger and wrapped him in swaddling clothes (for 15 minutes to two hours) which signified his future death as the Holy Righteous Lamb of God. An angel appeared to some shepherds and told them about the birth of **"a Savior, who is Christ the Lord."** The shepherds did not need instruction as to where to go to worship the baby, they knew because the baby ewes were born in "The tower of the Sheep" that the priest were in charge of. They were the sheep that were sacrificed in the Temple and the Shepherds were taught and instructed by the priest.

About six weeks later Mary and Joseph took Jesus to the

Temple for a purification ceremony. An old man named Simeon, who had been told by the Holy Spirit that he would not die until he had seen the Messiah, took Jesus in his arms and said, **"Now, Lord, you have kept your promise, and you may let your servant go in peace."**

While Mary and Joseph and Jesus were still in Bethlehem, some wise men from the East came to Jerusalem looking for the King of the Jews. They found him in Bethlehem **"with Mary his Mother"** and worshiped him and gave him gold and frankincense and myrrh. An angel appeared to Joseph in a dream and told him to take Mary and Jesus to Egypt because Herod wanted to kill the baby Jesus if he could find him. Just after they left for Egypt, Herod had all baby boys younger than two years old in the region of Bethlehem killed. Herod died, and Jesus and his parents returned a few years later, settling in Nazareth where Jesus grew strong and was full of wisdom. God's blessings were upon Him.

When Jesus was 12 years old, he went with relatives to Jerusalem for the Passover Festival. The family was evidently a large group because when everyone left after the festival, Joseph and Mary assumed Jesus was with the group. They traveled for an entire day before realizing that he was not there. When they returned to Jerusalem, they found him in the Temple talking with Jewish teachers. Mary said, **"Son, why have you done this to us? Your Father and I have been terribly worried trying to find you."** When they got back to Nazareth, the Bible says, he was obedient to Mary and Joseph.

Mary was at a wedding reception when Jesus turned water into wine. She was also standing near the tree (cross) when Jesus was crucified. To experience the Crucifixion through a Mother's eyes and feel it through a Mother's heart were as intense as any emotion she ever felt during Jesus life time. Jesus encouraged the disciple John to take care of her after Jesus died, indicating that she was probably a widow at that time. The last mention of Mary was after Jesus rose from the dead. He appeared to many of his followers a number of times and then went up to heaven. Mary probably witnessed his Ascension because she was among the disciples when they got together back in Jerusalem on Pentecost.

That's the picture of Mary in the Renewed Testament; that of a young girl, chosen by God to give birth to the Messiah. She was a loving and caring Mother who "treasured in her heart" her experiences and memories with Jesus as he was growing up. Wherever the Christian faith has taken hold, Mary has been honored, and each nation thinks of her and her child as its own.

Because of the lack of information in the Bible about Mary and the early life of Jesus, "Infancy Gospels" began to appear about 150 years later. They were attributed to Apostles and filled in whatever details people wanted to know about the time of Christ. The earliest were the Gospel of James and the Gospel of Thomas and were significant because of their effect on ideas about Mary.

Two thousand years ago, an angel appeared to a poor Jewish girl from a backwater town in Israel and announced that God had chosen her to give birth to the promised Messiah. Because of Mary's faith, her humble response of obedience, her life of purity and devotion, her godliness, but most of all because she "found favor with God," God greatly blessed her among women. She was more beautiful than Abigail or Bathsheba, stronger and more courageous than Esther or Ruth, a more remarkable mother than Hannah or Sarah and experienced more sorrow than Leah or Hagar. Mary treasured in her heart the memories and experiences she had with Jesus, for she was the source of his humanity, which God the Holy Spirit was the source of his divinity.

Elizabeth and Mary were Proverbs 31 women. Proverbs 31:25 says, "Strength and honor are her clothing, and she shall rejoice in time to come." Their sons were well known, accepted, celebrated and valued. Their words were life, hope, restoring and above all "redemption."

The Immaculate Conception
(As Told by Mary, His Mother)

We are on the way to the feast again, and camped near the Holy City. The road is thronged with people. Joseph's tent is near ours. I am so glad Joseph's tent is near. Oh, how beautiful the Temple is with the morning sun gilding it! City set on a hill, crown of all the nations.

One of the rabbis in the Temple today read from the prophet Isaiah about the wonderful child who was to rule upon a throne like David's, and of whose government there would be no end. How my soul kindled under his portrayal of coming glory! Through all her humiliation that hope sustains Israel.

We are on the way home. Mother asked me last night about Joseph, and I fell into her arms and told her I loved him. Then she said, "Joseph is a good man."

Joseph and I are betrothed. What beautiful days! Life passes like a dream. Joseph comes much to talk with father and mother about the hopes of Israel.

My heart is in a tumult. I tremble. I know not what to think; for as I walked along a sweet path near a fig tree an angel appeared to me and told me I was to be the mother of the Messiah. Seeing my confusion, he hastened to assure me; "And you shall call his name JESUS; and he shall be great; he shall be a King, like David; and his Kingdom will have no end."

"I am a virgin yet in my father's house and he is a priest," I pleaded; "it cannot be." "There is no cannot with God," the angel said, and vanished, leaving me alone.

O my soul; my soul is in ecstasy! Oh, words too large for my tongue to frame. Can it be? It cannot be! It is a dream! It could not come to one in such humble station. To be the *mother* of the Messiah; oh, that is an honor for only the rich and the great!

What? The secret of our nation between God and me! Shall I go up to Jerusalem to the High Priest? But I would be laughed to scorn. To whom may I go? Who would understand?

I yearned to tell mother this morning, but could not, it seemed so presumptuous, so unbelievable, yes, impossible. And Joseph, how can Joseph understand?

My secret oppresses me. If there was one to whom I could unburden myself, one who could understand!

I could bear it no longer and am on my way to Hebron to see my cousin Elizabeth. We have heard wonderful stories about Elizabeth. Perhaps she will understand, and give me protection. To her I may pour out my soul!

Elizabeth met me at the door, and before I had spoken she broke into rapture, calling me the mother of the Messiah and pronouncing blessings on me. It has been revealed to her, she said.

--

Three months with Elizabeth. Blessed days! We lived in another world, a world far removed from this, and unburdened to each other our bursting hearts. Two babes were to change the face of the world and those babes would call us *mother*.

I am leaving for home today. Farewell, Elizabeth. I am loath to leave; you only can understand. I must go now to the outside world, where explanation will be asked and no one will believe, perhaps not even mother.

Home in Nazareth. Joseph is coming tonight with his friend. I am afraid to meet Joseph tonight.

I fled to my room and wept. Mother came in and wept with me. I did not see Joseph. Mother tried to explain, but could not. He went away in great distress, while I lay under the heaviest burden womankind ever bears. O my God, time will vindicate me, but meantime what? I am troubled; my heart panteth; my strength faileth. Lover and friend hast thou put far from me; my friends stand aloof; my confusion is continually before me, and the shame of my face is covered.

Joseph is planning to send me away. How long wilt thou forget me, O Lord? How long wilt thou hide thy face from me? Consider and hear me, O Lord, my God; lighten my eyes lest I sleep the sleep of death.

--

Blessed be God; he has heard my cry. Joseph came to me, bowing low and imploring forgiveness; he made obeisance, declaring his unworthiness.

"Then you understand," I said.

"An angel appeared to me in a dream," he answered, "saying 'Joseph, thou son of David, fear not to take unto thee Mary, thy betrothed; for that which is conceived in her is of the Holy Spirit. And she shall bring forth a son, and thou shalt call his name JESUS; for he shall save his people from their sins."

Together we bowed in silence; then Joseph prayed brokenly: "Return unto thy rest, O my soul; for thou, Lord, hast dealt bountifully with us, and we shall walk uprightly before thee all our days."

Our wedding day, Elizabeth came, and her angel-promised child. Elizabeth and Joseph talked much together, and Joseph looked long into the face of her babe.

Elizabeth and Joseph and I are trying to understand the prophecies concerning the Messiah. We pondered over and over that Scripture that tells of a virgin that should bear a son and that his name should be called "God, with us."

Joseph looked tenderly at me and said, "It seems so plain now."

And we all know the rest of the story, only this is told through the heart and voice of Mary, Jesus Mother.

Matthew 1:18-2:15, Luke 1:26-56 and 2:1-52, John 2:1-11, Matthew 12:46-50, Mark 3:31-35, Luke 8:19-21, John 19:26-27, Acts 1:12-14

Proverbs 31

It is customary on Friday evenings after returning from the synagogue, that a Jewish man recites this hymn in gratitude for his wife and all she has done for him and their family throughout the past week.

Solomon may have written Proverbs 31 in memory of his Mother, Bathsheba. Some say Abraham wrote it as a eulogy for Sarah.

An excellent wife who can find?
She is far more precious than jewels.
The heart of her husband trusts in her and he will have no lack of gain.
She does him good, and not harm, all the days of her life.
She seeks wool and flax and works with willing hands.
She is like the ships of the merchant; she brings her food from afar.
She rises while it is yet night and provides food for her household and portions for her maidens.
She considers a field and buys it; with the fruit of her hands she plants a vineyard.
She dresses herself with strength and makes her arms strong.
She perceives that her merchandise is profitable.
Her lamp does not go out at night.
She puts her hands to the distaff, and her hands hold he spindle.
She opes her hand to the poor and reaches out her hands to the needy.
She is not afraid of snow for her household, for all her household are clothed in scarlet.
She makes bed coverings for herself; her clothing is fine linen and purple.
Her husband is known in the gates when he sits among the elders of the land.
She makes linen garments and sells them; she delivers sashes

o the merchant.
Strength and dignity are her clothing, and she laughs at the time to come.
She opens her mouth with wisdom, and the teaching of kindness is on her tongue.
She looks well to the ways of her household and does not eat the bread of idleness.
Her children rise up and call her blessed; her husband also, and he praises her:
"Many women have done excellently, but you surpass them all."
Charm is deceitful, and beauty is vain, but a woman who fears the Lord is to be praised.
Give her of the fruit of her hands, and let her works praise her in the gates.

7 Feast Of The LORD Being Symbolic Of New Life

Below is an overview of how the festivals of our Heavenly Father is liken unto new life.

Feast	Christian Fulfillment	Baby Development
Passover (Pesach) Fertilization must take place within 24 hours.	New Life (Egg) Leviticus 23:5	Ovulation
Unleavened Bread Matzoh Bread is stripped	The Seed (Planting) 1 Corinthians 5:7-8 Leviticus 23:6-8	Fertilization Christ buried
First Fruits Spring planting Leviticus 23:10-11; (Matthew 27:27-53; Early crop of believers)	Resurrection Resurrection Day Resurrection of the entire church	**Raised from dead**
Pentecost Acts 2:1-50 days from Reed Sea. 50 days Embryo becomes a fetus. Pentecost Greek word means 50.	Harvest	New Creature Fetus Sweet Holy Spirit

The 4 feast (festivals) above have been fulfilled at Pentecost. Christ breathed the Holy Spirit upon the disciples.

The following 3 festivals are unfulfilled. We await their fulfillment.

Feast	Christian Fulfillment	Baby Development
Trumpets 1st day of 7th month the baby can hear.	Catching Up (Rapture) Joshua 6:5 1 Thessalonians 4:16-17	Hearing

Feast	Christian Fulfillment	Baby Development
Day of Atonement 10 days into 7th month fetal blood changes so that it can carry it's own oxygen.	**Redemption**	**Blood** Hemoglobin A
Tabernacles End of Feasts Leviticus 23:27 15th day of 7th month Normal baby has 2 healthy lungs	**Kingdom** House of Spirit Spirit in the Air	**Lungs** Baby will live if born at Tabernacles

Hanukkah	**Eternity**	**Eternal Life**

Not given by God. A days' supply of oil lasted 8 nights. It's beyond Tabernacles and beyond the Kingdom. We have eternity with God. This is the fulfillment.

Job 23:12;

12 "I don't withdraw from his lips' command; I treasure his words more than my daily food."

Ecclesiastes 12:13;

13 Now all has been heard; here is the conclusion of the matter: Fear God and keep his commandments, for this is the duty of all mankind. (NIV®)

Bibliography

Hudson Publications, LLC
King James Schofield Edition
Jewish Bible
ABC's of the Bible

Made in the USA
Charleston, SC
01 June 2016